HIS MIRACLES OVERTAKE ME

By Linda Pendley

DEDICATION **5**

INTRODUCTION **6**
    WHY I WROTE THIS BOOK 7
    WHY WE NEED THIS BOOK 11

MIRACLES OF HEALING **18**
    HE HAS HIS DADDY'S EYES 19
    KATHRYN KUHLMAN AND ME 22
    FROM DEFORMED TO PERFECT 26

RAISING THE DEAD **30**
    THE HERMAPHRODITE 31
    THE FATHER OF THE BRIDE 33
    "UV MY DOG!" 35

SUPERNATURAL PROVISION **39**
    THE LEGACY BEGINS 40
    EGGS, MILK, & BISCUITS 44
    CROPPIE AND CORNPONES 46
    MORE EGGS IN 2007 48
    SPILLING THE TEA ON THE DEVIL! 50
    RACHAEL EASON 52

ANGELS **55**
    ANGELS AMONG US 56
    ANGELS ON A GEORGIA BACKROAD 57
    THE CANDY-STRIPER ANGEL 59
    LOST THINGS FOUND 64
    LOST RINGS AND THINGS 67
    THAT TIME MY FAITH WAVERED 68
    MOM'S SAPPHIRE RING 72
    ANGELS AT CHUCK E. CHEESE'S 73
    ANGELIC VISITATIONS 76
    DONNIE HAD ANOTHER VISITATION LAST NIGHT 79
    SUPERNATURAL BAND-AIDS 81

    DOTTIE RAMBO AND ANGELS WITH SCROLLS 83

SIGNS & WONDERS 90
    WHAT ARE THEY? 91
    THE WONDER OF BROTHER BIDDY AND THE ANGELS 92
    HEAVENLY CHORUS 94
    GLORY CLOUDS 96
    MINE EYES HAVE SEEN THE GLORY! 98
    GLORY IN A PRAYER [BED] ROOM 99
    MORE GLORY IN MY PRAYER ROOM 100
    SUPERNATURAL TRAVEL: BEING "TRANSLATED" 102
    MY FIRST SUPERNATURAL TRIP 105
    MY SECOND TRIP 107

DEFEATED DEMONS 112
    UNDER OUR FEET 113
    AN ANGRY DEVIL 116
    SHE VOMITED SLIME 118
    SHE VOMITED FROGS 120
    THE DEVIL HAS LIMITS 124
    BRENDA AND THE FORTUNETELLER 125
    I HOPE YOU ARE NOTICING A TREND 128
    FEAR HATH TORMENT—UNTIL MAMA GETS THE BROOM! 129
    MAMA AND THE KKK 132

DREAMS & VISIONS 134
    DREAMS AND VISIONS ARE FOR TODAY 135
    MY FIRST DREAM 137
    MY VISION OF HEAVEN 140
    THE MOVE IS ON 145
    UP IN THEIR BUSINESS 147
    CHANGES COMING FROM THE WEST 150
    ANOTHER DREAM AND VISION OF HEAVEN 152

PERSONAL PROPHECY 163
    GOD SAW ME PRAYING 164

LOOK OUT!	170
A MANAGER BY NEXT WEEK	173
"HELPING OTHERS IN STRANGE WAYS"	175
LET HIS MIRACLES OVERTAKE YOU!	**177**
MIRACLES EVERYDAY	178
LAST WORDS	183
ABOUT THE AUTHOR:	187

Dedication

To Donnie, I love you! You are my best friend. Your support and love are exceedingly abundantly above all I could ever ask or think.

Mom, I finished the book.

Introduction

Why I Wrote This Book

It began as a conversation with my mom. She always wanted me to write a book about the testimonies of miracles that have happened over my lifespan and hers—a legacy of the miraculous.

"People are going to be scared when troubles, trials, and tribulations come. They are going to need to know that God is still moving in mysterious ways, His wonders to perform." Mom's expression furrowed with concern in the middle of her forehead—it was in stark contrast to her normal jovial expression.

"You have to tell them about what God is still doing today." She urged, "You have to help them believe that God will still multiply food, send angels, raise the dead...you have to make them know that God is aware and cares about the things they care about. It is of paramount importance!"

When Mom used the phrase, "of paramount importance," she meant it. It was reserved for situations like when dad's appendix sutures burst open and he was refusing to go to the er. "Roland," she called Dad by his middle name, "You are getting in that car and we are taking you to the ER. It is of PARAMOUNT IMPORTANCE!" So, for her to pull that out of her lexicon to use in the context of writing this book I knew she was serious and had spiritual significance.

That's how it began. As I wrote this book, Mom and Dad were living with me and I was their 24/7 caregiver. Over and over, we experienced supernatural intervention during the seven years they were with me...and I was not ready to let them go. But as you'll read, the further along in this book I reached, the closer Mom and Dad came to their departure to heaven and when the time came for them to go I was not emotionally prepared. The Covid-19 pandemic had changed my expectations of surrounding them with family and love, singing and praising them into glory—that's what we had always talked about. When mom died alone in an ICU after being physically isolated from us for over a month, it was a devastating blow to my faith in God.

"How could he let that happen?" Every stage of grief was traveled through threefold as I wrote this book because Mom went first, then Dad, then my brother Donny who was a little more than 18 months my senior. It was a triple gut-punch and my faith wavered.

As you read, you may recognize grief in some of the words; you may sense the anger and questioning of God why things happened the way they did. I hope you do. You will see that victory comes from battles and that overcomers have literal obstacles to overcome. You will see that the sting of death is not for those who have gone on, but for those of us who remain to finish our own course. I sat the book down, stopped writing, and stopped almost everything but looking for answers to why. I got a job as a customer service rep (I'm very good at it) and put faith on the back burner.

But something was seared into my soul from my last real conversation with Mom the night before she fell and broke her ankle—the accident that started the cascade of events that took her. She made me look her in the eyes, "Buggy," Mom and Dad's nickname for me, "Finish the Book!" in that conversation I told her I was struggling to find a title, the working title I'd chosen was already taken. Without pause, she said to me, "His Miracles Overtake Me." It was sealed.

Everything that tried to crush my soul and keep me from writing the book and finishing the book, from that time to this, failed.

A Miracle Happened

My husband, Donnie, had been praying for me. He had to do it in his prayer closet because, when he'd try to get me to participate I would but the prayers I prayed were more like the Old Testament prayers. They came off like "...all day we are led like sheep to the slaughter..." and sounded like, "What is your problem? Where were the angels that were supposed to keep her from dashing her foot against a stone? Where were the ones that were supposed to keep and guard her and surround her with kind people instead of ones that would throw her medicine in the garbage in front of her because she asked for more water or applesauce to help her swallow them?" and those prayers were filled with rage. Judge me if you want to, but I am just being honest.

One morning I got up to log onto my shift and there was a malfunction and there was nothing I could do. So, I opened my personal computer, and there it was. **THE BOOK! OPEN ON MY COMPUTER!** Without thinking of how odd that was since I'd barely touched it for almost two years, I read it. The anger and questions in my soul faded to the background (they are still there but have grown "strangely dim"). I found myself weeping at God's constant faithfulness. Gratitude returned. Remembering him and his goodness returned. I returned to Him, a prodigal, wasting my life with the vanity of grief—he welcomed me with open arms.

That day I finished the book.

What to Expect from this Book

As you read it, I hope that your heart will explode in faith for God's supernatural provision. Mom believed that, if you read this book, you would begin to expect God to do miracles for you in your everyday life. She felt that, when you read it, you would know what to do when the circumstances of this present darkness tried to defeat you, a Child of the Highest God who is the Lord of Angel Armies. She believed that you would pray for the multiplication of food in your pot to feed your family when resources are low. She believed that you would grow closer to God in faith and that your children would read it and those prodigals would come back home to Him.

So, as much as this book is written by me, it is a legacy book of multi-generational miracles to encourage you that you are not forsaken and that the Lord is Good and His Mercy Endures Forever!

Love Y'all!

Linda,

Overtaken By Miracles

Why We Need This Book

It seems that, in much of the church, there has been a memory lapse that Christianity is, at its core, a SUPERNATURAL experience. It is experience-based, not in the five senses and the visible world, but in the unseen realms of the spirit.

> *"So, we don't look at the troubles we can see now; rather, we fix our gaze on things that cannot be seen. For the things we see now will soon be gone, but the things we cannot see will last forever." 2 Corinthians 4:18 (NLT)*[1]

Let's be logical. Without nuance, Christianity is based on a man being dead for three days and raised up from the dead. **That is not "natural"!** There is an entity called the Holy Spirit that we put our trust in to guide us daily. That is a basic tenant of the Christian faith. Even people who don't believe in the present-day baptism in the Holy Spirit with the evidence of speaking in tongues still believe in His existence. **It's not "natural"!** Jesus described God the father as a Spirit in John 4:24 and said that those who worship him must do so in *Spirit* and *Truth*. Again, **Not Natural!**

So, get it settled in your mind, the very nature of our relationship with God is a Supernatural/Spiritual relationship. Although there are experiences within our Christian walk that are in the realm of our five

---

[1] *Holy Bible: New Living Translation.* 2015. Carol Stream, IL: Tyndale House Publishers. As found in the Logos Bible study software program.

senses—sight, touch, smell, taste, and hearing—they are the most minuscule part of our experience. The greater part of our daily, Holy Spirit-led walk with God through his son Jesus is in the realm of the unseen. Jesus himself told us in John 15:19, "...you are not of the world...". So, if we are not a part of the world that we can see, what world are we a part of?

It's Natural to be Supernatural.

I have two words for you, Harry Potter[2]. It was and is still a global phenomenon. This series of books and movies showcase supernatural power, forces of light against forces of darkness, words having a supernatural effect, and humankind having the understanding and authority in an unseen realm. This tapped into people's natural intrinsic understanding that there is something beyond the five senses—not just children but adults as well.

According to the Pew Research Center, 63% of Americans believe that living things were created by a [supernatural] creator or that a supreme [supernatural] being participates in the evolution (ongoing adaptations)

---

[2] Rowling, J. K. Harry Potter and The Philosopher's Stone. Bloomsbury Pub., 1997

of living things.³ So why is the church that was birthed in the supernatural suppressing its very nature when people believe in the supernatural and are craving to experience it? It is BONKERS!

Seeker-Sensitivity=More Miracles Please!

First let me qualify everything I say about the Church with this: I love the church. I'm a part of the church. I don't criticize pastors of little churches or mega-churches based on their style of preaching or liturgy. I've been in ministry for over thirty years, and I know that the sermon you see on a telecast does not encompass the canon of teaching that is brought at a church. I know the good and the ugly about televangelists from firsthand experience. There are good'uns and rotten'uns. My stance is that the Lord knows how to handle his kids without my input other than to be the one who intercedes for mercy for them and their families. I don't get to talk about ministers and ministries more than the time I have invested in them in prayer. So, my talking about ministers is mostly a vertical conversation between the Lord and me.

I am, however, very aware that the church's modern theology in general, under the guise of "Seeker-Sensitivity," has often gutted the Gospel of its spiritual and supernatural core. This has caused the mod-

---

³ Science In America: Religious Belief and Public Attitudes." Pew Research Center, 2007, https://www.pewresearch.org/2007/12/18/science-in-america-religious-belief-and-public-attitudes/.

ern church to be a form of godliness while denying its power (2 Timothy 3:5). This is an error that diminishes our relevance to this generation who is craving supernatural experiences.

What are the Numbers?

As I began researching the beliefs and values of our modern generation, I found another Pew Research poll that said that almost 65% of Millennials pray DAILY, even those who don't attend services regularly.[4] This should be a wake-up call to the church. This generation is more spiritually centered than previous generations, however, they are not as connected to the religious centers that are supposed to teach them the power of the Word of God. We've been calling them snowflakes, melting away at any little heat when in fact it is the church that has been melting away in relevance because we've tried to present an inoffensive, non-controversial church to a generation that thrives on offense and controversy. It makes no sense! They crave the supernatural, and we dole out psychobabble. They want to see miracles and we want services to work like machines.

---

[4] " Religion Among the Millennials." *Pew Research Center's Religion & Public Life Project*, 2010, https://www.pewforum.org/2010/02/17/religion-among-the-millennials/.

> *"Tick-tock, watch the clock*
>
> *And you will be a good pastor.*
>
> *If the deacon taps his watch,*
>
> *Then preach the sermon faster."*

The gospel (good news) itself is **the power of God unto salvation** (Romans 1:6). Salvation power is supernatural power. Ephesians 1:21 tells us that it is the same as the resurrection power that raised Christ from the dead. Supernatural! So, to be truly seeker-sensitive the church should put its full supernatural nature on display.

Let me throw this scripture out there for you to chew on for a sec. The Apostle Paul wrote:

> *"Yet I dare not boast about anything except what Christ has done through me, bringing the Gentiles to God by my message and by the way I worked among them.* **They were convinced by the power of miraculous signs and wonders and by the power of God's Spirit.** *In this way, I have fully presented the Good News of Christ from Jerusalem all the way to Illyricum" (Romans 15:18-19)*[5]

---

[5] (KJV) Bold, italics, and underline mine.

Hmmm? They were convinced to serve God, not just through preaching, but through demonstrations of power in miraculous signs and wonders by the power of God's Spirit.

I know some people will look at this book and say that it's controversial and provocative—left or right of the mainstream. Yet, in reality, this book is "seeker-sensitive" to the seeker of the supernatural aspect of the church of the Lord Jesus Christ—which, statistically, is the majority.

I've seen too many miracles, experienced too many encounters with both angels and demons, had too many prophecies, dreams, and visions come to pass, and had too many prayers answered to water down or be ashamed of the Supernatural Gospel of Christ

The Wake-Up Call

We need more power, more anointing, and more demonstrations of the church as written in the book of Acts. We need to be the "more than conquerors" that Romans 8:37 talks about. That cannot be done with a stripped-down patty-cake religious form.

Revelations 12:11 tells us that we overcome the power of Satan by two things: the Blood of the Lamb, and the Word of our Testimony. How does that work? Well, the more we talk about the supernatural intervention of God the more people's faith grows and the more we give room for God to show up and show out in the way He has always done throughout his Word.

From Genesis to Revelation and every bit of eternity before and after that, God's supernatural Glory is evident–manifesting to mankind. He's not changing his method of operations just because the clock ticked, and the calendar shifted. His supernatural kingdom is still active, and we can tap into it—to live in it. This book is just a little nudge to your noggin and a spark to your spirit to help you believe, so you experience His Supernatural Assistance.

Miracles of Healing

A survey from the Pew Forum on Religion showed that a vast majority of Americans, nearly 80%, believe in miracles. [6]

"I don't just believe in them. I've lived in them, experienced them, and seen them with my own two eyes." Linda Pendley

---

[6] " Religion Among the Millennials." *Pew Research Center's Religion & Public Life Project*, 2010, https://www.pewforum.org/2010/02/17/religion-among-the-millennials/.

He Has His Daddy's Eyes

I was just a kid when I saw my first miracle. We had this man in our church who was born blind but not the kind of blind where he had eyeballs and irises and pupils. Nope. He had NO EYES and where his eyes should have been, there were two little things that looked like snail antennae. I loved that he was in our church because he would bring his seeing-eye-dog to church, a big German Shepherd. I mean, how cool could you get to be able to pet a dog during church services?

One Sunday morning we were having one of those Pentecostal services where the organist, Bro. Biddy would play and whoop and holler and shout (there is a story about him coming up in the section on signs and wonders). One of the songs that would tear the house down and set the roof on fire was Hymn number 294 in the "Melodies of Praise" Hymnbook, "Victory in Jesus!" The first verse was:

"I heard an old, old story

How a savior came from Glory

How he made the lame to walk again

And he caused the blind to see" (E.M. Bartlett)

Something about that day and that anointing was electric in the air. Dad, who was the pastor of our congregation of about fifty people, got

---

[7] "Victory in Jesus". Words and Music by E.M. Bartlett© 1939 - Administrated by Integrated Copyright Group, Inc. All rights reserved.

to the pulpit and preached the present-day power of the name of Jesus. Deeper Life Tabernacle's faith went through the roof and the blind man with the dog made it to the altar at his mom's side.

Dad took him by the head and screamed, "In the Name of Jesus!!!!"

The man started blinking and shaking his head, "Something is happening!" He said, astonished, "Something is happening!"

After about five minutes dad stuck his thumbs in the empty holes, "I SAID, IN THE NAME OF JE-SUS!" Then he lifted his thumbs and investigated the sockets, "He's got eyeballs!" He seemed as shocked as the blind man himself.

The man turned towards his mama, "I can see a light." He said. She screamed and covered her mouth, "Don't be tricking me. Don't be tricking me!" She could hardly believe what she was seeing.

The Holy Ghost hit Bro. Biddy again and he hit some licks on that Hammond B3 organ that came from heaven's music room.

Dad put his thumbs back on the man's closed eyes and grunted out the words, "In the name of Jesus," as if it took great effort to lift them out of his guts. Then he stepped back again and looked, "Open your eyes now." He spoke gently this time.

When the man opened his eyes, he had the most crystal blue irises. He jumped back and screamed and closed his eyes, "I wanna see my mama!" He kept his eyes closed until they stood him face to face with his mama. When he opened his eyes she screamed, "You have your daddy's eyes! Those are your daddy's blue eyes!"

That place went nuclear. Bro. Biddy played "Victory in Jesus" and the whole church rang to the rafters with the chorus.

I was so happy he could see his mama. As a little'n who loved her mama, that really touched me. But the next Sunday believe me, I was saddened about him getting his sight back...because he didn't bring his dog to church anymore.

Kathryn Kuhlman and Me

It had to be that same year around 1974 or '75, that Kathryn Kuhlman came to hold a crusade at the Shriner's Auditorium in Atlanta, GA. I know this because I am exactly 3 years 361 days older than my baby sister, Brenda—she came home on my fourth birthday. She was still in mom's arms in a blanket when this happened.

Kathryn Kuhlman's Atlanta visit was controversial because she had her meeting in the Shriner's Auditorium. In those days, Christians having a meeting at the **SHRINER'S AUDITORIUM** was tantamount to having church in a brothel. This was because the Shriners were known for two things, their Children's Charity and orgy-like conventions. The religious consensus at the time was *Kathryn Kuhlman was a "woman preacher"* it just figured she'd break all propriety and do something like that. I assume the truth is that she had the meeting where she could rent a building. Women in ministry was still a great taboo and churches created great obstacles for them to overcome.

That's how many church people felt and talked back then—so religious, so bound by traditional views, so anti-Christ (against the Anointed One and the power of His anointing). If they had only looked to the Bible to see that the Apostle Paul preached at Mars Hill, a place of many temples to various gods, Greek and Roman, introducing the Athenians to the Unknown God, Jehovah, through Yeshua (Jesus). The anointing is in the people of God and then they take it into the place where the gospel is to be preached. The anointing goes where his people go. Ok, let me hop off my soap box and get on to the testimony.

Mom was carrying my sister, Brenda, in her arms. I was wearing my best pink dress and pinafore holding onto her long black maxi skirt as we crossed the parking lot. We were walking towards the auditorium, my brothers, Donny and Billy, 6 and 7, were holding my Dad's hands, and my sister, Paula who was about 13 at the time, was walking ahead of us wearing a pink chiffon knee-length dress.

There was a large crowd of people doing the same thing we were, walking toward the building. The atmosphere was strange, encompassing...heavy. Not a heaviness from the hot Atlanta summer, but a weightiness of the presence of God. My brother Billy looked up at Dad and whispered, "Daddy! God is here."

Whispered exclamations of awe were the only sounds other than the rustling of clothes and the *clink clank* of wheelchairs and walkers, crutches, and leg braces. A holy hush covered the property that would be broken only by whispers off, "God is in this place," or "God is here," or "Ah, Jesus," all in muted, reverent tones. His tangible weighty presence in the atrium of the auditorium was heavier than the parking lot and the actual auditorium felt like static electricity flowing over my skin. My brother, Billy whispered, "I can breathe in here." His chronic asthma could not stand in the healing presence there.

I sat on the metal folding chair and watched as an older woman rolled a younger man into the aisle in front of us. He was quadriplegic and had tubes in his nose, mouth, and running out from under his red and black buffalo-checked blanket. I don't know what his diagnosis was, but his wheelchair was not typical, it was more like a chair on a hand truck. I was mesmerized by all of the accouterment that was connected to him and how the lady was so attentive to him. I have always assumed she was his mother but I was a four or five so anyone over 18 was old to me. She just as well could have been his sister or wife.

The lights went down and the music started. I don't know who was on the piano or who was singing but the song was, "How Great Thou Art!" Sister Kathryn was wearing a flowing blue chiffon dress and doing little twirls on the stage. I watched her cottony red hair glisten in the light and marveled at how much she looked like my great-grandmother, Mom-Mom. Then the song was, "Spirit of the Living God, Fall Afresh on Me"

The weighty blanket of the power of God began to shift and move. It felt like ocean waves of warm oil. Every hair on my body stood up. At that moment I looked at that piano player and prayed to God, "That's what I want. I want to play the piano for you like that."

Sister Kuhlman pointed at our section, "Up there! My Friend, Holy Spirit is moving up there!"

Suddenly there was a sound that went through that place like a crack of lightning that hit above my head. The fellow in the wheelchair started grabbing tubes and yanking them out of his body. His caregiver was trying to get him to stop, but he pulled out a catheter, and he wasn't wearing pants under the blanket. She kept trying to cover him but he was determined he was coming up and out of that bondage of sickness.

Sister Kuhlman, still pointing at our section, "Oh, Holy Spirit! I Believe. I Believe!"

The man was soon standing out of his wheelchair, free from all the tubes wrapped in the red and black buffalo-checked blanket. "I'm healed!"

People surrounded him and the music lifted in a great crescendo of bold glisses traveling up and down the piano. I said it again to God, "That's what I want to do. I want to play the piano and people get healed." I felt that electric power hit me in my stomach and overtake me like warm oil. I received that anointing and to this day, when I play the keyboard the Spirit of healing comes and people receive their miracles.

From Deformed to Perfect

To Preface, the following, the account I am giving is not just from my mother's account but also of others who were there and told me from firsthand knowledge including my Granny K, mom's Aunt Barbara, one of the women who worked with mom at the salon, and the lady who helped rescue Mom and Paula.

Both of my parents have children from previous marriages. We don't call each other "half" anything, I just have sisters and brothers. My mom's first marriage was a forced marriage. Her dad had died when she was fifteen and Granny K fell apart. She lost herself in the cocktail culture of the late 1950s. She was a woman, alone with an empire of businesses to run and devastated by the loss. Mom was a teen girl who was dealing with her own grief and the two clashed.

To make a very long and nuanced story short, my Granny K dressed my mom up one day and took her to a place where she married her first husband. She didn't even know she was getting married that day. She hadn't taken the required blood test or had any preparation. She had the clothes on her back and a tiny blue samsonite travel case. She was sixteen. Granny K signed two contracts, one was giving Mom's new husband a beauty salon, and the other was permitting him to marry the underaged girl. Mom begged her not to sign. Everyone in the room laughed at her.

The marriage was loveless, and she worked as a slave for no wages at the salon. The only times of "intimacy" between her and her husband were when he was very drunk, and they were always violent. She became pregnant at 17.

While working 18-hour days at the salon mom was not allowed to eat because her husband said she was getting fat. He knew she was pregnant but would not let her get too big for her clothes. She would sneak off and eat a candy bar, drink a soda, and smoke cigarettes. She worked six days a week at the salon. One of her customers gave her a radio. She hid it in her bag and took it home. She began listening to preachers on the radio when her husband would leave for the night, leaving her locked in the room with no food or water.

In April 1964 when my sister was born, she was a dry breech birth. She was completely deformed with clubbed feet and cleft palette and the doctor said she was "mentally retarded" because her head size was small compared to her body. She also had lump on her neck that connected her head to her shoulder. They didn't expect Paula to make it. Mom would feed her by dipping a cloth in milk and sugar and having her suck it off of the cloth because she couldn't suck from a bottle, mom was too malnourished to breastfeed.

Mom asked her grandparents if she could come and live with them and bring the baby. Her grandmother, MomMom, said yes, but DadDad said no because they were still raising Granny K's youngest at the time and didn't have room.

Mom lost hope. When she got Paula home from the hospital, she decided to take a razor and kill her and then use the same razor to commit suicide. It was Sunday and she was locked in her room. She had been given a TV and she turned it on to drown out the sound of

Paula crying when she slit her throat. When she did, Oral Roberts was on the television. He said clear as day, "Little mama, don't hurt that baby. Don't kill yourself. Jesus is calling you to him today. Won't you accept him? Won't you let him deliver you out of bondage?"

Mom dropped the razor and fell to her knees sobbing. She prayed the prayer of salvation with Oral Roberts. At the end of the telecast he mentioned that they would be having communion and that anyone could take part.

The beatings became worse when her husband found out that mom had prayed and accepted Jesus. He used electric cords, belts, fists, boards, furniture and the entire time he would say things like, "Can Jesus save you from this?" Mom said it was the only beating she never felt. She looked at him and said, "You can try to kill me, Devil. But I'm not giving up Jesus."

On the Sunday that the communion service was supposed to happen her husband beat her with the electric cord from the tv and threw it in the lake. But mom had memorized the time and a friend had snuck her a letter from MomMom with a communion wafer in it talking about the communion service. Mom took this as a sign from God. At 12 pm on that Sunday afternoon she went into her room and locked the door. She laid Paula on the bed in front of her and took off her blanket and clothes. Paula lay there, jerking uncontrollably because she had no real control of her body. Mom had snuck a half a shot glass of wine from the liquor cabinet. She took the wafer that MomMom had sent her. Then she drank the wine. "I remember you, Jesus. Now you remember me."

The lump on Paula's neck was the first thing to disappear. Next her club feet began to pop and crackle and contort. Suddenly her legs were long and straight with two beautiful feet connected to them and 10 perfect little toes wiggling and flexing. Then Paula let out a sound, when her mouth opened mom could see a beautiful pink pallet and her perfect tongue resting behind a strong gum plate. Her misshapen head rounded out and grew and her eyes that never really focused on anything suddenly focused on mom. She smiled and reached for mom's nose. It was the first connection Paula had had with anyone.

Paula could read when she was 3. At 17 she was a model—I am talking fabulously beautiful! She has been the founder of several multi-million-dollar organizations that do great outreach for Christ in marginalized communities. She is married to a wonderful man, Bill, and they have four children that are all highly intelligent and beautiful.

Paula is a miracle walking every day.

Mom said this about Paula, "She was worth every pain. The miracle of her was worth every sorrow of uncertainty. I cannot take communion without remembering the miracles of that day. Little Suzie-Q (Paula's nickname) made communion a living breathing expression of the body and the blood—the sacrifice instead of the sacrament."

Raising the Dead

The blind receive their sight, and the lame walk, the lepers are cleansed, and the deaf hear,
*the **dead** are **raised** up, and the poor have the gospel preached to them. (Matthew 11:5)*

The Hermaphrodite

There was a time when my parents owned a nursing home. They cared for mostly hospice type patients and those who were a danger to themselves with problems like dementia or Alzheimer's disease. Many of the elderly people in mom and dad's care recovered through prayer, a good diet and actually went home to family, many of them went on to be with the Lord peacefully. But then there was the one...

That person had lived the bitter life of a hermaphrodite, having been born with both male and female genitalia. The Lord and that patient only knows the suffering they went through over their lifetime. Dad, when he speaks of the person says she (that's the assignation the doctors gave her) was to be pitied.

She cursed God every day for making her the way she was (stupid religious people tortured her emotionally with that lie). Dad witnessed to her the saving, healing love of God and His miracle working power to her every time he came into the nursing home. He had faith for her healing, and a compassion for her bitterness of soul. He had been raised with a child that had been born with the same malady. The child was raised as a girl until she was ten or so when a "faith preacher" came through, laid hands on her and all her girl parts disappeared. After that, he grew up, got married and had a bunch of kids.

Unfortunately, this patient was bitter at God and didn't want anything to do with Him and cursed Him foully at every turn.

Dad came in one morning to find the head nurse was making her rounds and she mentioned in passing that the lady had passed away and they were waiting on the mortuary to come and get her.

"NO!" Dad said to the nurse in anguish, "She hasn't accepted Jesus. She's in hell!" He ran to the room where the dead body lay. The Nurse was holding dad back from the body and telling him that it was all right, and it was the natural progression. "There's nothing you can do, Mr. Robinson. She has been dead for over an hour."

Dad laid his hands on the cold body and yelled, "Death, I rebuke you, in Jesus' name, God give her one more chance to repent and receive you!" He called her name and told her to "Come back to your body, NOW!"

She suddenly gasped and screamed the blood-curdling scream of a tormented soul coming out of hell. She opened her eyes, and they were full of fear and pain. Then she locked eyes with my dad in total awareness.

"You died and went to hell." Dad told her. You can go to heaven, just ask Jesus into your heart."

She snarled and let out a line of curse words towards God with her last breath and slipped into eternal hell screaming.

The head nurse stood there trembling in shock at the miracle she had seen.

The Father of the Bride

It was a beautiful wedding. The blushing bride was walked down the aisle by her father and married her dark-haired, hippie looking love. I had turned the pages for the piano player during the ceremony, so I was on the platform looking down at the wedding. I remember the bridesmaids wore large brim hats with flowers on them and the flowers were daisies and sunflowers. It was a normal 1970's flowerchild looking wedding until the bride's mom screamed, "He's Dead! Oh, God No!"

My dad threw down his wedding book and ran towards the pew where the bride's father sat slumped and blue around his mouth. His eyes were bulging, and his tongue was sticking out. He had a heart attack during the ceremony and was completely dead. They laid him back and dad yelled for someone to call an ambulance. (this was before the days of cellphones and 911 but the ambulance station was right up the street from the church on Moreland Ave. in Atlanta, GA).

Then Dad screamed, "NOT TODAY! OH NO, DEATH! YOU ARE NOT RUINING THIS GIRL'S WEDDING DAY!"

The mother of the bride hysterically said, "He's dead. It's too late, he's dead!"

Dad took him by the lapels and yelled, "You come back here, now, in Jesus' name! Death I rebuke you, in the Name of Jesus. This man shall LIVE AND NOT DIE!"

That went on for a few minutes and the EMT's came in with a gurney. They told dad to step away, "Preacher, you can see he's long gone. Leave him alone and let us get his body out of here."

Dad got down in the face of the dead man, "Death, I said I rebuke you. You are not taking this girl's daddy on her wedding day, In the name of Jesus, WAKE UP!"

The Father-of-the-bride took a gasping breath and blinked. "I'm ok." He kept reassuring his daughter and wife. "I'm ok." The wife almost fainted. The daughter collapsed into a pew praising God and crying. The EMT's jumped backwards in astonishment. I did too. The man went with the EMT's and then wound up at the reception to send his daughter off on her honeymoon.

I was seven or eight when this happened, so it was June of 1977 or '78.

"Uv My Dog!"

God loves people. God cares about things that concern us—even our pets.

Sam was in his mid-forties, but his cognitive function was that of a toddler. His mother, Mary, had taken him out of an institution back in 1974 in order to bring him to church for dad to pray for him. That was around the same time that the Lord gave the blind man eyes.

Sam only had one emotion, it was a strange smile. He was non-verbal and slobbered constantly. He had gotten caught in the womb at birth and had brain damage. He walked, but in strange jerky movements and was unsteady. Dad laid hands on Sam at that time and prophesied to him and his mother. "He will grow up. He will care for you in your old age. By the time you go to heaven he will be self-sufficient."

On the outside this was impossible. His mother took the prophecy on by faith and did not return her forty-plus-year old toddler to the institution but took him home.

Sam went through his terrible twos, throwing tantrums, learning to use the potty, learning to speak words. A grown man throwing tantrums like a toddler is a strange sight. He had little cars he carried in his pocket to play with. He wanted to run and play with us kids. I was a little snobby about it, but my little sister, Brenda was ever patient with him. She was six and he was pushing fifty but she had a way to talk to him and teach him things. Sam started learning to tie his shoe, it was a line of stacked knots, but he did it himself. And he finally became verbal. "I hungry" "Uv [love] God" "My Car" "My room."

He would dance and praise God at the front of the church and testify every testimony service, "Uv [love] God," but he only said it because that's what everyone said, like a baby mimicking his mother.

Sam went through "puberty" and had crushes on every girl he saw but still had only the mental capacity of around a 5 to 7-year-old boy. He started working at a little store bagging groceries and bought rock n roll records at the thrift store with his own money. He loved music.

Sam was beginning to have more and more connection to the real world. He began to learn to read. His mom and he talked about it, and he wound up buying a small dog and named him Christian. Christian was Sam's responsibility and his best friend.

Christian brought out maturity and true emotions in Sam. Sam began to understand "Uv".

One day Sam opened the door to take Christian out for his morning walk. There was a dog across the street and Christian bolted away from Sam, ran out into the street and was hit by a car. Sam screamed. Sam ran inside crying to his mom, "Dog dead, mama! Dog dead!"

Mary ran out to the street. The man who had hit Christian had stopped, but Christian was flat in the middle and his bodily fluids were squished out. Mary picked Christian up in a towel and wrapped him up. Sam was inconsolable. "Mama! Dog dead!"

Mary held that lifeless squished dog and said, "Sam, let's pray for Christian." Then she prayed, "God, I know Jesus didn't die for a dog, but he did die for my son. I'm asking you to bring Christian back from the dead for my Sam. You love Sam."

Suddenly the lifeless form in Mary's arms screeched and jumped up and into Sam's arms. They took Christian to the vet and, although he was covered in blood, they couldn't even find a scratch.

The next Sunday in church Sam got up to testify. He didn't have that strange grin on his face. He had tears in his eyes and used a pointed finger to make his point as if he were a preacher, "Uv God." He said matter-of-factly. "Uv my dog!" He punctuated his testimony with his finger. Then he turned towards his mother and for the first time in his life uttered the words, "Uv mama!" I was sitting one row in front of her and turned to look at her as he pointed at her. She fainted at the words she never even hoped to hear, "Uv Mama."

Y'all, I have to tell you that I am sobbing trying to write this. As a mom, to have never heard one of my children tell me they love me would be heart breaking. But then, through a miracle God gave me not only the gift of bringing a dog back from the dead, but hearing my child tell me they love me!? It gets my guts every time I think about it.

When Sister Mary gasped and crumpled in that floor from hearing those words...I can only say that joy overtook her.

When she got up from fainting, she told us the testimony of Christian being raised from the dead. She started singing a song that brings great joy to my heart every time I hear it since that day, "OH Love of God. How rich! How Pure! How Measureless, and Strong! It shall forevermore endure— the saints' and angels' song." That was in 1984. I was fourteen.

Sam went home and broke up his rock n roll records because he "Uv God" more than his music. He bought Gospel albums after that. He continued to grow mentally. By the 90's he was taking his mom on cruises with the money he made on his job. He was able to take care of her in some capacity as she got older with the help of his older sister. Then, by the time Mary went to heaven in 2014 in her 90's I've been told Sam was able to care for himself with assisted living care.

SUPERNATURAL PROVISION

"We have here only five loaves of bread and two fish," they answered. "Bring them here to me," he said. And he directed the people to sit down on the grass.

Taking the five loaves and the two fish and looking up to heaven, he gave thanks and broke the loaves.

Then he gave them to the disciples, and the disciples gave them to the people.

They all ate and were satisfied, and the disciples picked up twelve basketfuls of broken pieces that were left over.

The number of those who ate was about five thousand men, besides women and children.

Matthew 14:17-20 (NIV)[8]

---

[8] The Holy **Bible**, New International Version. Grand Rapids: Zondervan House, 1984. Print.

The Legacy Begins

There have been several times in my lifetime that the Lord has multiplied food. I will tell you that this is a legacy miracle in my family. To my knowledge it started back in the great depression with my maternal great-grandmother, Kizzie "MomMom" Sedman. She was married to the most stubborn 4'11" man on the planet, Clyde "DadDad" Sedman. He had been the foreman of the hosiery factory in Chattanooga, Tennessee but someone did something that made him mad. He walked out of his job and never went back to it. He had a family to feed. At this time in history men were begging for work riding the rails on cargo trains across the country looking for any kind of work so they could send money back to their pitiful wives and starving children. Although the history books say that the depression ended in 1939, for many of the industrial cities the depression continued into the first few years of World War II and beyond. With the men off to war many families lost their primary source of income as soldier wages didn't always compare to day wages. Chattanooga was one of those cities where the depression lingered into the early1950s.

My grandmother dropped her Irish twins (children born a year apart or less) off at MomMom's so she could continue her work in Philadelphia at the shipyards. Two more mouths to feed along with their own children still living at home. My mom, her older brother, and eventually their younger brother all lived there on meager rations. Food was often hand to mouth. They were struggling.

On this particular day, MomMom looked through the house for something to cook for BabeBabe and Bub's meal (my mom and her not-so-much older brother).

She found two little homemade beanbags used for tossing and kids' games. She snipped the sea, poured the beans into a flour sieve to run water over them, and tipped them into a little pot. Mom said it yielded about a cup of beans.

MomMom pinched a little salt in it and went to the hoosier-cabinet and sifted out her last bit of flour, took her last spoon of bacon grease, the little bit of buttermilk left over, and made two little biscuits. A welcome rain began pattering on the roof. MomMom was grateful that she had a roof over her head. She told Bub and BabeBabe, we have to be thankful because there are people who don't have a roof over their heads and they are out in the rain. She got Bub and BabeBabe ready for lunch when a knock came at the back door. She saw what they would call a hobo or transient. He looked like a down-on-his-luck fellow who had walked from the railroad tracks looking for a handout, soaked to the bone.

MomMom took Bub and BabeBabe and put them under the kitchen table, "Now, babies, you hush and listen. We may be entertaining angels unawares."

The man came in and sat at the table. MomMom took his boots to dry by the wood-burning stove. Bub and BabeBabe sat under the table listening to the conversation. MomMom served the man a plate of beans and both biscuits. She didn't make a plate for herself because there was not enough for herself and the children too. He bowed his head before eating and he blessed the meal and the household and brought the kindness of this little lady to God's attention. Then MomMom and the Hobo talked about God and his faithfulness. MomMom asked the man where he was from, "Not too far away." He answered vaguely. Then he continued with his discussion about God and his faithfulness with emphasis on the widow who had fed the prophet and her barrel of flour and cruise of oil "failed not." As he sat there eating and talking to MomMom the rain was creating a mud pit in the backyard where the Hobo had come through to the back door. It was a sloppy mess. Just as the Hobo finished eating the rain stopped. He put on his boots and thanked MomMom. Then he stood and turned to the back door. He looked back over his shoulder at MomMom and said, "You will never go hungry again."

He stepped down the back steps.

MomMom called Bub and BabeBabe out from under the table, "Quick, quick, come see!" They ran to the back door looking out across the muddy yard for the man. She pointed down to the ground at his boot prints. There were three steps deep in the mud then they disappeared.

MomMom turned, and with her wry smile, she walked over to the hoosier and started turning the sifter. Flour poured out. She made a full pan of biscuits with bacon grease and buttermilk. She dipped beans out for Bub and BabeBabe and a full bowl for herself. They ate till their stomachs were full, and DadDad came home he ate a large bowl and biscuits. Her two children still at home came home and ate their fill. The lady across the street came over and asked to borrow some flour. MomMom filled up a large bowl for her. The other neighbors heard that MomMom had flour one by one over the next few weeks, and sometimes more than once, people would come to borrow flour. MomMom never refused anyone who asked. She kept her miracle to herself. "How did you get such fine flour?" they asked, "Your ship must've come in!"

Often people would bring a cup of sugar, a bag of potatoes, carrots, onions, some bacon, or a chicken breast to trade.

The angel's declaration was true. MomMom, Bub, and BabeBabe never went hungry again in their lives to this day.

The miracle of the flour and grease and buttermilk lasted for months until DadDad brought home a bag of flour, "Kizzie! I figure you must be about out of flour by now." He said as he proudly poured the fifty lb. bag into the hoosier, "We sure fed a lot of people on the last one, didn't we?"

MomMom was sad that the miracle time had ended. But it made a big impact on BabeBabe (my mom), and, by legacy, myself.

Eggs, Milk, & Biscuits

Dad was a fiery preacher who didn't teach on tithing, Mom was a preacher's wife with four kids at the time this testimony happened, in the early 70s. This was the dark-ages when preacher's families were often kept on poverty wages. Over and over God had to give the Robinson family miracles of provision of food. It was also the time where the husband would bring home guests without notice.

When those three things converged—no money, no food, unexpected guests—Mom had thing where she would just smile a wry little smile and go into the kitchen to prepare something.

On one occasion a ministry family came through with four children when Dad was out of town preaching a Revival. So, let's count, 5 Robinsons and 6 guests. That's 11 people and mom had 3 eggs, a little flour, a little lard, some milk, and a bit of bacon. She announced that everyone would be having breakfast for dinner. She went into the kitchen and said, "God, you said that we should be given to hospitality. You sent us guests today, and you need to feed them. You said that shame would be far from me, and I would be very ashamed not to be able to feed your servants as they have come through our city to visit us."

Then she scrambled some eggs, made a pan of biscuits, cooked up the few strips of bacon, and put the milk in a pottery pitcher so that no one could see how very little was there.

She put the eggs in a bowl and covered it. She did the same to the biscuits and bacon.

With eleven people sitting at the table mom brought out the bowls. The guest minister blessed the food. Then mom held the bowl for him to dip out eggs for himself. He dipped out two **BIG** spoonfuls. Then she handed him the biscuit bowl, he reached under the towel and grabbed two. He picked up the pitcher and filled his glass and then took four pieces of bacon. By mom's count everything should have been gone except three biscuits.

BUT!!!!

The bowls passed around to the guest family and they all filled their plates, then our plates filled up. We talked, and laughed, and ate and ate and ate. Mom never said anything about it as she sat there eating and smiling and laughing just like the rest of us. At the end of the meal, everyone bragged on Mom's eggs and biscuits. It was the best meal they'd had in a long time. The preacher ripped the towel off of the eggs and the bowl was full as was the biscuit bowl full of leftovers. There was a full plate of bacon. The milk had poured out into glass upon glass, satisfying thirst and yet was still full—fuller than it had been at the first.

It was years later when that family returned, still bragging on that meal that mom had made.

Croppie and Cornpones

This happened again later when the same family came through. Dad was home this time and, ever given to hospitality, invited them in. Our cupboards were still bare and the dad of the family came in bragging, "We had a choice between going out and spending money on a great big spread or coming here! Guess what we chose?"

Dad had gone down to the little wash-way with a kid's pole and some worms he dug out of the yard to get catch us a meal. He called those fish "silver-dollar" fish because they were a little bigger than a silver dollar. He'd caught a few, but not enough for the crowd that was noisily taking over the living room, stretching out and making themselves comfortable.

Mom made her way into the kitchen. She looked at her ingredients and began to thank God again for his faithfulness. She reminded him that the reason that family was in her living room and hungry was that His word commanded us to be "given to hospitality."

This time mom had some corn meal, milk, an egg, and those crappie.

She used the same faith that had worked before adding, "You don't want to embarrass your children and make us look like we need to beg for bread, do you?"

Mom confessed to me that this time she was more than a little perturbed at the family for coming in town unannounced. She felt it was rude, and the dad had bad manners, chewing with his mouth open and talking while he had a mouth full of food. These things were one of mom's greatest pet-peeves. Also, the man never allowed his wife to participate in conversation. She was mostly a silent mouse who smiled a tired little smile and always agreed with her husband. Mom pitied her and was willing to give the woman a break from being in the car with her husband and loud children. Their kids played with us kids outside 'till dinner was complete.

Mom covered the food with towels and set them on the table, with a pitcher of milk. She called us all in and we sat , with Dad at the head, he blessed the food. He gave the visitors first dibs, and they filled their plates to overflowing with the largest meatiest crappie you've ever seen, some of them as big as tea saucers.

Needless to say, the food multiplied and fed twelve people and again there were leftovers. Dad did not realize the miracle, but he did mention that he didn't remember catching such big and so many fish. Mom didn't enlighten him. Just like MomMom she kept her miracle close to her heart, reminded of the scripture, "Be still and know that I am God."[9]

God was faithful then. Faithful to Mom as the legacy of her grandmother and the miracle continued.

---

[9] Psalm 46:10

More Eggs in 2007

Did you know that you can make too much money to get food stamps and have no groceries in your house to feed your children even in the new millennium. That was me. I had two kids to feed and only three eggs in the refrigerator. I had a second challenge, my kids hated eggs. I went into the kitchen and planned to scramble up the eggs and believe God for a miracle of multiplication...but they said they'd only eat over-easy. I put the carton on the countertop beside the stove and took out my "over-easy" pan. I had a pat of butter and some salt and pepper. I had some milk.

I said to myself, "God is the same yesterday, today, and forever!"

Ok, I hear you growling under your breath, "You should have made your kids eat what you had and not played into their pickiness."

Let me reason with you. If you knew that your kids would go hungry until lunch time at school the next day and then they would only get a cheese sandwich and a low-fat milk because you didn't have finances to buy them a good school lunch you would make something for them to eat that they would actually eat. That's what I did.

So, I reached my hand in the carton without looking singing a little praise song to God:

> "Great is thy faithfulness. Great is thy faithfulness;
>
> Morning by morning new mercies I see.
>
> All I have needed Thy hands have provided.

Great is thy faithfulness, Lord, unto me."

    I cracked an egg and cooked it, salted it, flipped it and slid it on a plate and gave it to my daughter. She was seven. Then did it again for my son. He was six.

    By time my son got his, my daughter wanted another. I reached in without looking and found an egg, cracked it and went through the process. Then my son wanted another one. So, I reached in the carton without looking, but thanking God for his provision, "All I Have Needed Thy Hands Hath Provided!" My hand hit an egg, I pulled it out, cracked it and served it up. My daughter wanted another, and by that time their daddy had come home, hungry. I didn't blink, I just reached into the carton and kept pulling out eggs and making them over-easy for my family until they were full. My husband had eaten four, my daughter three, my son three, and I ate two. That is a full dozen eggs. When I put the carton back in the refrigerator there were still three eggs in it.

    God provided for the kids' school lunches, he blessed us with groceries and provided in many ways that I will testify about later in this book.

Spilling the Tea on The Devil!

My parents lived with me for seven years until they passed within 2 and a half months of each other in 2021. That was just two months ago as I write this line. I was their 24/7 caregiver. Not too long before Mom's passing, Mom ran out of tea. She drank it with her morning toast, and it was a need for her in order for her to get her pills down. So I went to the empty box and said, Lord, you love my mom. She needs her tea to help her swallow. Then I stuck my hand down in the box and two teabags appeared in my hand. TWO!

Why it's a big deal?

Would you believe it? The very day I started writing this book my husband was released from his job. I didn't have money for teabags for my mom. I'm telling you that this book is a threat to the Devil. We overcome the enemy by the blood of the lamb and the word of our testimony. You see that it isn't just Jesus conquering the Devil by his blood, but it takes us using our testimony —telling the story of what the Lord has done for us—to put the Devil in his place—To OVERCOME him. The Webster's 1828 Dictionary defines "overcome" as:

- *To conquer; to vanquish; to subdue; as, to enemies in battle.*
- *To surmount; to get the better of; as, to difficulties or obstacles.*
- *To overflow; to surcharge.*
- *To come upon; to invade.*
- *To gain the superiority; to be victorious. Romans 3:4.*

So, if you think about it, the Devil is trying to overcome us! You can see by this testimony, he's trying to subdue, surmount, or get the better of me.

Not Today, Devil!

I'm writing this book needing a miracle. I'm writing this book feeling a bit overwhelmed by circumstances. I'm writing this book with a lot of unanswered questions but this one thing I know; God has been faithful so many times before, and he has not changed. My feelings have nothing to do with God's ability. By writing this book and giving my testimony I am overcoming the enemy by the blood of the lamb and the words of my testimony.

Hupernikao

I'm going all "Hupernikao" on the Devil's hind-quarters! Romans 8:37 in the King James Version calls us "more than conquerors". That entire phrase is trying to describe one Greek verb, "Hupernikao." Paul was actually saying, "In all of these things we are **_perpetually, actively victorious_** over our enemy right now!" Think of it like using an atomic bomb to kill a spider. That is our current level of victory over the devil.

You see, these testimonies of supernatural provision are not just the past, but they are the present and the future of the people of God. They are available to me. I still need them. They are available to you. They are available to your children. In the next chapters you'll find more faith building testimonies of the supernatural. Let them build your faith in God's supernatural provision.

Rachael Eason

This woman has a crown in heaven! When Mom visited heaven, she said that she saw givers wearing shining robes that distinguishes them from others. I am certain Rachael Eason is undoubtedly wearing one of those shiny robes.

There were times in my childhood when our family had run out of earthly resources. We were sitting in the dark until dad could scootch finances around to get the utilities covered. It was stressful. Rachel would show up on our porch on Vernon Ave, in Atlanta, GA with an envelope of money, a bucket of KFC, and a smile. She didn't even attend our church! She was just a woman who listened to God and was willing and obedient. In today's terms, she would be considered "special needs" or "other abled" because she was not very intellectual. Her conversations were simple in terms of vocabulary and subject matter (i.e., It rained last Tuesday. My flowers grew. My family is doing good). She could drive, live alone, garden in her little garden, and take care of her personal space and personal hygiene. She was the sweetest, kindest, gentlest, goodhearted, person. She oozed the fruit of the Spirit.

Rachael Eason would be standing at the door with her simple smile and coke-bottle glasses and say, "God sent me."

I want to reference her in this book by name so that, while she may be gone on to glory now, her contribution of obedience and giving to meet the need make her worthy of people on this earth speaking her name in gratitude and awe—striving to be a willing and obedient part of the body of Christ.

God Providing at Thanksgiving through Rachael Eason

When the cupboards were bare in our home, they were BARE. One year when I was about 12, we came up on the Thanksgiving season during a very hard patch. We (5 siblings, 1 nephew, Mom, and Dad) woke that morning to the smell of nothing. Mom was in the kitchen banging around looking for the Turkey platter. We all got a glass of milk and the baby had some baby food but thanksgiving dinner was nowhere to be seen. We kids were sure that there would be no turkey, dressing, gravy, or mashed 'taters.

Mom lifted her eyes from digging in the back of the cabinet under the countertop stove, "Have you seen the turkey platter?"

"Did we get some money?" I asked, bending down to help her find it.

"No." She felt in the darkness for the cold of the porcelain platter with a little grunt and a smile as she brought it out, sending pots clanging around in the cabinet.

"Did we get food?"

She smiled at me, "It's coming. Let's set the table."

We knew that look on mom. She didn't have any plan but to trust God, and he had never failed. She made us get dressed up (people used to dress up in Sunday Fancy clothes for holiday meals) and set the table. She kept the same wry smile on her face as we would question what we were going to eat.

"What do people normally eat for Thanksgiving?" She put it on us to imagine what was going to be on that table.

Noon came, and that was our regular time to eat Holiday Meals. We all sat at the table, dad at the head and us all around, the good plates in order before us, and the good "silver" all shined and ready for use. Mom walked to her chair and started to sit when a knock came on the door. She stood up and went to the door. It was Rachael Eason with an entire fully cooked Thanksgiving dinner. Her family had gotten snowed in and couldn't make the drive and she had cooked for an army of people.

Mom made us kids help Rachael bring in the paper Winn-Dixie bags full of already cooked food and groceries that Rachael had bought for her family to be there for the week. She didn't even stay for dinner. She just smiled her strange smile, waved her Rachael Eason wave, turned, and left.

Let me encourage your heart, you may be the one in need or you may be the one who the Holy Spirit is tugging on to take part in God's Supernatural Provision to others. If you are on either side of this grace, God is able to do exceedingly abundantly above all that you can ask or think according to the power that worketh within us[10]. God will use either side to show his mercy and grace. He is just that good.

---

[10] Ephesians 3:20 (KJV)

Angels

Are not the angels all ministering spirits (servants) sent out in the service [of God for the assistance] of those who are to inherit salvation? Hebrews 1:14 (AMPC)[11]

Be not forgetful to entertain strangers: for thereby some have entertained angels unawares. Hebrews 13:2 (KJV)[12]

---

[11] *The Holy Bible: The Amplified Bible.* 1987. 2015. La Habra, CA: The Lockman Foundation. As found in the Logos Bible study software program.

[12] The Holy Bible: King James Version. Dallas, TX: Brown Books Publishing, 2004.

Angels Among Us

As you read in the testimony of MomMom and how God gave her a perpetual miracle of food that sustained her entire neighborhood for months, there was a visitation of an angel involved. She was keenly aware that the man that came to her back door was not merely a man. The above scripture, Hebrews 13:2, came to her thoughts as soon as she saw the man begging at her back door.

God still sends angels to us in this modern age for us to extend to them hospitality, thereby obtaining our needs met, our questions answered, our breakout or breakthrough, our next assignment, or our miraculous supernatural provision. The testimonies that follow will encourage you to know that the angels are working on your behalf, to recognize them when they appear, and to know how to act when you come face to face with a minister of light. They rarely show up in white flowing robes with a halo of glory shining around them, they usually look like mere mortals, but there is a something about them, a peacefulness in their atmosphere perhaps, a knowing comes on you and you just recognize that the Lord has sent your answer in the hands of angels.

Angels on a Georgia Backroad

Mom and Granny K (her mom) were traveling down an old Georgia back road in the mid-60s. Back then the roads were two lanes paved, maybe there would be a center line, maybe not. The roads were lined on either side by miles and miles of tall Georgia pines and kudzu-covered hills and trees.

Mom was about 19 at the time and a single mother, my sister, Paula, who was a toddler at the time, was with them. They were on their way home from a revival. There was hardly money for food, they had enough gas to get from one little South Georgia town to the next and that was it. Along this desolate stretch of road, they had a blowout. The tire burst and it was a miracle in itself that the big heavy Lincoln they were driving didn't flip. Granny K pulled onto the side of the highway. They had not seen anyone or anything for ten miles at least. Before the despair of being stranded in the South Georgia heat for "Lord only knows how long," hit them and before they could cry out to God, a pickup truck pulled in behind them with two of "The sexiest men I've ever laid eyes on" to quote Granny K. "They had dark tanned skin, brownish black hair, wearing dungarees (jeans) and T-shirts over their broad shoulder muscles."

The men came and asked them if Mom and Granny K needed help. Then they took the tire off the car. As they worked in the stifling, humid heat, mom and Granny K both thanked them, "Y'all are an answer to prayer. We cried out to God, and you showed up. You're an answer to our prayers."

The handsome young men took the tire and slung it into the back of the pick-up truck and said they'd be right back.

They left and less than fifteen minutes later they came back with a new tire and a bottle of chocolate milk for Paula. They replaced the tire quickly.

Mom and Granny K tried to give them a few dollars for their help, and they refused. "It is our pleasure, Ma'am." Their smiles beamed with charisma. "We'll follow you out to make sure you get going." they said, waving, before getting in their truck.

Granny K pulled back out onto the road and started driving with the truck in her rearview. As promised, they followed behind her. Mom kept looking back as Granny K drove. There were no side roads, no tree farm roads, no houses, no exits, just miles, and miles of hilly roads and Georgia pines and kudzu. The Lincoln-full of grateful women went over the crest of a hill and lost sight of the truck. When they started going up the next hill there was no truck behind them. It had disappeared.

Mom said they each burst out in laughter not wanting to tell the other that they thought the men were angels from the beginning, nervous the other would think them crazy.

They traveled that road over and over each time they came to those hills looking for a place where the truck could have disappeared or the service station they could have used. Even years later, when we would go on that highway mom would point to the place where Angels changed her tire and brought Paula chocolate milk then a few miles down the road she'd say, "That's where they vanished."

The Candy-Striper Angel

In 2003 Granny K was just about ready to go home to Jesus. Her health was failing, she was suffering from mini-strokes almost daily and they were taking their toll on her abilities to function. We (my mom and I) were keeping and caring for her at home in shifts. She had home health to come in once a week, at that time they didn't do daily care for a homebound patient, that was left to mom and myself. Granny K always had a fear of being put in a "home." Mom and I didn't want that for her either. So we worked together to keep her with us as long as possible.

One day I was at home with Granny K and she died. She had no breath nor pulse. Something inside me knew it wasn't her time. I called 911 and then I called my parents who were at a doctor appointment for mom. The paramedics and my parents arrived at the same time. I left her bedroom and pulled my kids into the kitchen to explain to them what was going on. The paramedics called me back into the room to ask me a question about Granny K's DNR they had on file. I gave them the paperwork that said she did not want any special measures taken, but I asked them to please try. One of them took her pulse and shook his head, "We'll take her to the hospital, they'll pronounce her there."

"Lord, she hasn't finished yet. Mom's not ready to let her go. Granny K, wake up." I said under my breath beneath the noise of their dispatch radios and clanging of the gurney and equipment.

They lifted her up onto the gurney. I don't know why they had the gurney up so high because her in-home hospital bed was not as high as the gurney was set. They started to walk and suddenly the gurney dropped from being up high to almost flat to the ground.

Granny K opened her eyes wide and gasped, "What are these sexy men doing in my bedroom?" Granny K was a lifelong flirt and even though she was in failing health, she still had the beauty to back it up.

There were four paramedics in her room, two from the fire department and two from the ambulance company. All of them let out a startled yell. They turned ashen. It was hard not to laugh.

At the hospital they discovered that she had a urinary tract infection that made her urine thick like syrup and opaque yellowish green. The cure was a high dose antibiotic that made her hallucinate. This was the third time she'd had it, and her doctor refused to let her come home with us. The cause was probably due to her kidneys beginning to fail (they did not diagnose this, they only treated the symptoms). Although we were giving her excellent care, her need of constant medical attention and not just physical caregiving had overtaken our abilities.

There was only one place that Granny K said she would go to if she ever needed to be cared for beyond our abilities, Baptist Village.

Baptist Village is the premier assisted living facility in South Georgia. I knew one lady who lived there for over thirty years. She never had a bed sore, she never smelled of that old and dying smell. Her family swore by their care.

Granny K had been the lady's hairdresser for years and knew that Baptist Village would not mistreat her. However, there was a catch.

Baptist Village had a waiting list, as you can imagine. People make reservations years in advance in order to be there. We had made no such plans.

When the doctor refused to release Granny K to our care, mom and I sat in the hospital room and blinked at each other numbly. The hospital social worker came in with paperwork to send Granny K to the only place with an opening. Its reputation was epically horrendous, from maggots in bedsores, to sexual assault by other patients, and physical abuse of the patients by staff. It was bad.

Mom had tears streaming down her face and she shook her head, "I won't sign that. Give me one day to see what else I can do." She insisted.

The social worker shrugged the shrug of someone who knows that there is no sense in arguing. It was late in the day so one more night wouldn't make a big difference.

Mom stayed with Granny K that night at the hospital, she and Granny K talked about it and Granny K said that she wanted to go to Baptist Village. "If they can't get me in there, just push me out the window, cause either way I'm finished. I'm a dead duck."

Early the next morning Granny K was still asleep, and mom was sitting at the little table in the room when a hospital volunteer, a pretty young lady wearing the traditional candy-striped apron, peeked into the room, "Mrs. Robinson, call Baptist Village right now. Don't wait. They have an opening and if you wait, you'll miss it. Fill out this paperwork and take it to them. Don't delay."

"What?" Mom asked her, shocked at the inside information. The Candy Striper told her who to talk to and what to say specifically. Mom wrote it down, thanked her, and turned to pick up the phone to call dad to come take her right then. She suddenly wondered what the volunteer's name was so she could thank her. Mom opened the door and looked up and down the hallway to find her. The nurse at the station across from Granny K's room asked mom what she needed.

"The little candy striper that just came into my room, what is her name?"

The nurse looked at her like she was crazy. "What's a candy striper?"

"A hospital volunteer in the little red and white striped pinafore." Mom explained.

The nurse laughed, "Our hospital volunteers wear peach scrubs and have a hospital Volunteer ID card."

"Oh." Mom was beginning to suspect an angel, "What about the young lady that just came out of this room. Where did she go?"

The nurse shook her head, "Mrs. Robinson, I don't know what you're talking about. I've been sitting here for the last thirty minutes. No one has gone in or come out of your room. Are you okay? You must have had a dream."

Mom nodded and apologized for disturbing her. The papers in her hand let her know that it was no dream. It was God's angel bringing the answer to her prayer. She went back into Granny K's room, filled out the paperwork, took it directly to the administrator at Baptist Village who the angel instructed. The woman looked at the papers and looked up at mom, "Where did you get these?"

"A candy-striper at the hospital gave them to me and told me to bring them to you right now that there is an opening. I didn't get her name"

She nodded, "Yes, that's true, there is an opening, we were about to call the people on the waiting list. Whoever gets their paperwork in first gets the spot. You got here before we made the call. That is so strange."

Granny K spent the last three months of her life in Baptist Village, mom going almost every day to care for her personal needs and the staff taking care of her medical needs. She went to heaven on January 25th, 2003, after an evening of singing worshiping God and telling mom everything she needed to hear so they both could have peace with her going home. In the section about dreams and visions, I'll tell you about me seeing Granny K in heaven and what her home looked like.

Lost Things Found

I was taught by my mother from a very young age that lost things can be found with the assistance of angels. She often would lose her keys or misplace her purse. Why? She had five children, was the principal of a large Christian school, administrator of a Bible college, and coordinator of our Friday night youth outreach that brought in about a thousand youth every week. She did this all while co-pastoring the church. She was always in demand and didn't have an earthly assistant. In this earthly realm she was kind of on her own with the day-to-day stuff, so things would get misplaced but in the heavenly realm, she had angelic assistance—assistants that worked overtime on her behalf.

So often Mom would stand in the middle of the dining room and say aloud, "Ok, Angels, I've lost my keys, put 'em where I can put my hand on 'em." She'd have us keep looking and she'd walk around looking and we'd turn around and there they were in the middle of the dining room table, or in her empty coffee cup she'd just sat down from drinking the last sip. Once she reached into the freezer to get some ice, stuck her hand in the ice bucket, and pulled out her keys. They always showed up in the most improbable places to let us know that it was the Angels who put them there. Sometimes, they didn't show up immediately with the lost item. Mom would smile her wry smile and say, "The Lord must be saving our lives from a car wreck or setting us up for a blessing or something. He is delaying us for a reason." Without fail, we would see the wreck or accident, or we would be set up to some divine appointment because of the delay.

It wasn't just the keys. She did the same thing with her glasses, her purse, her kids...pretty much anything that was displaced and needed to be found. She would send angels to gather them and bring them to her. To think about it now, it is the ultimate way to "cast your cares on the Lord" (Psalm 5:22; 1 Peter 5:7) by utilizing the kingdom of God's supernatural assistance to act in a crisis rather than sit idly by as a victim of circumstance.

Because of these life lessons of sending angels of which we saw results almost daily, it was a part of the Kingdom Way that I didn't really study for its theological soundness. It was just a part of our life. When people with theological training started in on me to tell me I was wrong about the function of angels within the Kingdom of God I paused and considered their argument. Some of them said that angels were "for messages from God to specific people for a specific time for a specific purpose." I agreed.

Others would add angels are "announcers of prophetic times and seasons." Yup! That too!

When someone would finally get brave or snarky enough to ask me, "Who do you think you are that you think you can command angels to find your keys?" I was able to answer them this way,

"I am a child of God, an heir according to the promise. The Word of God declares to me the righteousness of God in Christ Jesus[13]. I am seated with the Father in heavenly places where God intended for me

---

[13] 2 Corinthians 5:21

to be. The angels are in awe of this and talk about it among themselves[14]. So, it is not beyond the pale that if the Father is seated above them in authority, as a child of God, I am seated with HIM above them[15]. The Bible says that angels are here to help me on my journey[16], so, they can help me find my keys this morning. They can go before me to protect me or set me up for success, favor, and the blessings of God in my day down here."

Friend, I don't want the angels who the Lord has assigned to me to not live up to their full potential. They are waiting for us to put them to work. They want to "hearken to the voice of God's Word."[17] Hearken means to "hear and do." So, anything that gets us closer to fulfilling God's will in our lives or reaching our full potential in the Kingdom, the Angels are listening for nothing more than us needing their assistance and telling them what they can do to help us. Finding keys are a little thing but when you get confident about keys you can be confident about putting them to work on other things like keeping your kids safe, You can be confident that your faith-filled prayers are actually working because of the success you've seen in the little things.

---

[14] Ephesians 1, 3, 5; MSG, AMPC, and JUB

[15] Ephesians 2:6

[16] Hebrews 1:13-14

[17] Psalms 103:20

Lost Rings and Things

I loved my wedding set. 18 little diamonds set in 14k gold. I'm sitting here thinking about how my husband, then boyfriend, Donnie, gave them to me. They were in his glovebox in that little black F150 when I got back to Oklahoma from an evangelistic trip to Missouri. He had called me while I was away and asked, "What would you say if I asked you to marry me?" I said, "I'd have to pray about it, but I would say yes unless God said no." His reply was sharp and to the point, "He's not saying no, so you're going to marry me." That was his full proposal. My reply was, "You're getting a virgin..." I was 28 years old and had saved myself for marriage, "...so I expect diamonds." I wasn't kidding but I knew he wasn't made out of money, so I expected a little chip on a 10K ring.

Imagine my surprise when I opened the glove box, I saw the ring box and took it out and opened it. There were 18 diamonds on my wedding set and 14 on his matching ring! He didn't get down on one knee he just asked me while I was looking at it, "Well, aren't you going to put it on?"

God made that man just for me. He knew that I didn't want syrupy platitudes, I wanted stability and kindness, and real "think about you before me" love.

That Time My Faith Wavered

After we were married but before we knew more about living in the kingdom principles and living by our faith, we got into some sticky situations financially. The Lord would have helped us more, but we just didn't feel like we could ask him. I know it is dumb to say, it is an even dumber way to live but we just didn't know back then what we know now.

We had two babies who needed food, and our cupboard was bare, bare, bare. We didn't even have beans and rice. I was having a pity party, so my faith wasn't focused on Gods supernatural ability to provide.

Don't judge. We all slip in faith sometimes and get weary during the battle. This is just one of those time in my faith-journey that I wasn't at my best.

I chose to break up the set and sell my engagement ring at a pawn shop to buy groceries. I'd never been in a pawn shop. I know now I was stupid. They gave me less than $100 for it. It felt like I was selling my guts, it hurt so badly.

A few weeks later I realized that somewhere at some time my wedding band had fallen off my finger. THAT WAS TOO MUCH! I had no clue where it could be. I searched high and low, deep cleaned the car, the house, the drains...everywhere I could think of. It was gone. I felt so sick.

I took a cheap costume ring from Walmart and wore it on my left ring-finger. I told my kids, "Mommy has lost her ring, but the angels are going to go get it and put it where I can find it. I'd have them help me tell the angels to go find my wedding ring and put it where I could put my hand on it."

It was missing for several weeks. I don't know why it took so long this time, my faith had been renewed that they would bring it back. I knew that ring would show up and that the Angels were working on it. I would even touch my fake ring and say to God, "Lord, thank you that your angels are out there getting my ring and putting it where I can put my hand on it. I know you're working on something big!" And I'd tell my kids, "God is doing something big. It's going to be so cool when my ring shows up! It wouldn't take this long if he weren't up to something."

So, one nondescript morning I got up out of bed and went to take a shower. I took off my little Walmart costume ring and put it in my jewelry box ring drawer. I had made the mistake of showering it on once and it had turned my finger all shades of black and gross. I said my little confession, "Lord, I thank you that the Angels are working to find and bring my wedding ring back to me today and they are going to put it where I can place my hand on it."

I took my shower, got dressed, went to the jewelry box and mindlessly picked up my costume ring that I'd placed in there a few minutes earlier. When I did, I felt more than one ring in my fingers. I slid my fingers around hearing the metal slide against metal and feeling the sensation as I looked down! There on my finger was the cheap Walmart costume ring, and my wedding band!

How God Resurrected my Choked-out Faith

There were several things going on at the time. Our church started a series on "the Ministry of Angels" leading up to Christmas. So, although my faith had wavered on God's Supernatural provision for food, as the Word of God was preached, I was bolstered in my faith. Romans 10:17 says, "...faith comes by hearing, and hearing by the Word of God." (KJV)[18]. I really like The Passion Translation of that verse which says, "Faith, then, is birthed in a heart that responds to God's anointed utterance of the Anointed One." (TPT)[19] As I began to be immersed in God's word about the ministry of angels again, the experiences and testimonies from my childhood began to thrive again. I had allowed the cares of the world to choke[20] out the word I'd learned as a child, and it took the preaching of the word to renew my faith in God's Supernatural Provision.

I began having faith that my ring was going to show up. I had no outward clue how it would happen. I did my due diligence and searched. I

---

[18] Scripture taken from the New King James Version®. Copyright © 1982 by Thomas Nelson. Used by permission. All rights reserved.

[19] The Passion Translation®. Copyright © 2017 by BroadStreet Publishing® Group, LLC.

Mark 4:19 (AMPC) Then the cares *and* anxieties of the world *and* distractions of the age, and the pleasure *and* delight *and* false glamour *and* deceitfulness of riches, and the craving *and* passionate desire for other things creep in and choke *and* suffocate the Word, and it becomes fruitless.

prayed and thanked God that the angels were bringing my ring back to me and putting it where I could put my hand on it, but I didn't just come up with that outcome out of the blue. I was overcoming that doubt because I had seen God do it before.

Mom's Sapphire Ring

My mom had lost the main stone in a very expensive sapphire ring. This ring was one she wore daily and received many compliments on because it was as elegant as she was. We were traveling on the road as evangelists at the time. It could have been anywhere from the Keys of Florida to Connecticut, or as far west as Arizona! On the ring, the stone is considered large, but in a 40ft travel bus, that sucker was tiny. She started saying the same thing I said, "The angels are going to put my little stone where one of us can find it and put our hand on it.

There was this purse that no one had used in probably over a year. One day I decided to switch my things over into it because I suddenly thought it was a cute purse.

I reached my hand down into clean lint out of a corner and when I pulled my hand out there was the sapphire in my hand.

Angels at Chuck E. Cheese's

During the same time as my lost ring unseen Angles assisted me again.

My ever-popular son, Stephan, was invited to a classmate's Chuck E. Cheese's birthday party. It was a big deal for him. The invitations said that food and tokens (back when they used tokens) were for the invited guests only. There was one problem, I had to get him there and pick him up, and I only had enough gas to do that once. So, Mackenzie (Kenzie) and I had to go hang out and eat with NO MONEY or just sit there and watch everyone else have fun. That made me mad. Not at the parent for setting parameters, they weren't being mean at all. They were on a budget as well. No, I was angry at not having provision for my daughter. I didn't care about eating pizza and playing games. But to have my daughter sitting there just one year older than my son having to watch the other kids play while she is left out? *NOT TODAY SATAN!*

I started saying, "Kenzie, we are going to that party, and the angels have already gone before us and prepared the way for you and you will have more fun than anyone, you won't be left out. You're coming home with more prizes than anyone." I repeated that same phrase, "The angels have gone before us and prepared the way..." over and over across the time of the week leading up to party night.

I had scraped together four quarters for 5 tokens and handed them to Kenzie. "This is just to get you started, the angels have gone before us and prepared the way for you to have the most fun of anyone."

When we arrived, Stephan went with his friends and Kenzie, and I got her 5 tokens and I found a seat to watch. She went to a machine where you win tickets by trying to get the light to land on jackpot when you push the button. IT STOLE HER TOKENS!!!

I was livid at the devil and some Chuck E. Cheese's employees! *You ain't gonna steal from my baby.* "NO, NOT TODAY SATAN!" I growled through gritted teeth under my breath, but in my spirit, I was screaming with authority.

Because confrontation is not my first nature, I think I scared my daughter and the little teenager with the key to the machine when I said, "That thing stole from my daughter. I want her tokens back!" Rather than replacing the tokens from behind the counter—the easy fix—he, instead, walked me over to the machine, opened the mechanism and fiddled around with it for a second and two tokens dropped into his hand. He handed them to her and shut the machine and turned around to leave. The machine started lighting up like something from Vegas and coins started spewing out of it into the floor. The teenager with the key turned around in shock, "That has never happened before." He gave Kenzie a LARGE cup to put them all in. We stopped counting at 100 tokens because she didn't want to waste time counting, but there was almost triple that amount. PLUS the machine spewed out an entire roll of tickets. The teenager let her keep them. ALSO, everywhere Kenzie went in the Chuck E. Cheese's, people—adults and kids—would come over and drop more tokens in her cup or give her more tickets. She was a token/ticket magnet.

Because Kenzie is such a giver, she was going through the arcade dropping tokens in machines for everyone.

People kept coming up to me and asking me about my girl and complementing her kind heart. I was able to testify to several people about the goodness of God that day and prayed with the birthday-girl's mom for God's goodness to be revealed in their lives too.

Someone gave Kenzie a pizza, another party gave her ice cream, and cake and even a trip to the salad bar.

Kenzie had the most fun. She came home with the most ticket toys. She gave more than she used. And she testified to everyone when they asked, "how'd you get all those tickets?" She answered, "The angels went before me and prepared the way for me."

That day was the epitome of the scripture, "...Him who is able to do exceedingly abundantly above all that we ask or think according to the power that works in [us]." (Ephesians 3:20, NKJV)

I love The Passion Translation of this Scripture:

> *"He will achieve infinitely more than your greatest request, your most unbelievable dream, and exceed your wildest imagination! He will outdo them all, for his miraculous power constantly energizes you".*
>
> *(Ephesians 3:20, TPT)*

Angelic Visitations

Some people think you have to be a prophet to the nations to have angelic visitations. I don't think you should seek one. We should look to the Father, look to the Word, honor to the Son, and yield to the Holy Spirit, that is what is important. However, I do know that angelic visitations are for anyone who needs one. Paul tells us to be given to hospitality because we may be entertaining angels unawares [21].

I can tell you this, angelic visitations **always** precede life-changing events. It's as if they are there to flip the switch of our current life track and put us on another track completely. They show us that the transition from one season to the next is in the works and that from this moment on things will never be the same.

You can see clearly that the Scriptures bear witness to this with just a little bit of digging. When you type in the word "Angel" into your KJV bible app you'll find 108 Old Testament hits and 175 New Testament hits on the word. In every situation where an angel showed up, there was a change in the circumstances, life direction, or probable outcome. Suddenly, impossibilities became possible, the unlikely became certain, and promises from God were fulfilled; victory, breakthrough, divine protection, supernatural physical strength, wisdom from the

---

[21] Hebrews 13:10

throne of God—all of these happened when the Lord of Hosts sent an Angel.

This has been true of every Angelic Visitation in my family's life as well. One visitation I want to tell you about is one my husband had. Now, let me preface this by telling you that he was not raised like I was. Donnie's spiritual upbringing was not religious. His mom taught him that God created the world, Jesus is the reason for Christmas and Easter, and that you need to be a good person. He became a Christian in his late teens and struggled in and out of church for a bit. Compared to my "daily-in-the-temple" upbringing it seemed a bit "desert" to my "rainforest." However, he didn't have all the religious theological hangups and his "simply believe" faith was a lot easier to live than mine. So when he called me one day from work and said, "I just fed an angel...I think." I was like, "HUH!?"

"Yea, a man came in and asked me for lunch. I just kinda knew he was an angel and I comped his meal"

"What did he [the angel] say?" Of course, I was wary because I thought that I was the spiritual one to whom God would send the angel.

Donnie: "He said he was a Colorado Cowboy and was talking about stuff out west."

Me: "Colorado?"

Donnie: "Colorado."

Me: "What was an angel doing in Colorado? Are you sure he was an angel?"

Donnie: "Pretty sure."

In the fifteen years since that day, I still haven't gotten much more out of Donnie than that about the encounter but right after that our lives took a drastic turn. He was promoted at work. We moved from Waycross, GA to Fort Worth, TX. We became members of Eagle Mountain International Church, the place where we learned so much more about the Kingdom and the daily walk of faith. He and I finally got on the same page, spiritually. We changed tracks with that angelic visitation.

Donnie Had Another Visitation Last Night

Last night I was asleep and felt the presence of something in the room with us. I opened my eyes, and the room was still and dark with only a faint blue light from the alarm clock illuminating Donnie's nightstand. My eyes looked in that direction and I knew an angel was standing over Donnie as he lay sleeping. I didn't see it with my natural eyes, but my spiritual eyes saw the angel very clearly. I kept blinking my natural eyes because my spiritual eyes were seeing so clearly, more so than my natural ones. It was as if the spirit realm was superimposed over the natural realm which shifted to the background as a lesser reality.

The angel stood about seven feet tall and had a hooded robe. It was not like the grim reaper, but it was more like a gothic monk whose robe was shining like glass. The angel had no wings. He looked down on Donnie with an expression of curiosity and peace, his head cocked toward his left shoulder. The angel acknowledged me with the slightest of nods and continued to look over Donnie while radiating strength.

I sense that I could have said something. I could have asked the angel why he was there, but I left him alone, only laying there and watching him study my husband intently, continuing to blink at the darkness while seeing the light of the spirit realm in the foreground.

My mother had told me the day before to expect more angelic activity as I write this book and as the pressure mounts to quit and let it go.

I asked her why. She answered, "The angels always come with strength from the throne of God and provision in the time of need when we are doing the will of The Father." She didn't give me a chapter or verse to confirm this, but she mentioned Elijah being strengthened by angels in his time of greatest pressure[22] and Jesus was strengthened and fed by the angels at His greatest times of pressure, the Wilderness of Temptation[23] and the Garden of Gethsemane[24].

At this visitation, we realize the tide of this war of spiritual suppression has turned. Our breakthrough is at hand. What that is going to look like is yet to be seen.

---

[22] 1 Kings 19:5-8

[23] Matthew 4:11, Mark 1:3

[24] Luke 22:43

Supernatural Band-aids

When I was in my early twenties and living in Louisiana, I took a trip to Atlanta, GA to take care of my sister's four children while she and my brother-in-law went on vacation. They were good kids, so I didn't have to worry about them giving me any trouble. The only one that I worried about was little Mikey because I was told he "liked" to fall and hit his head on things. So, I kept a close eye on him.

Mikey didn't have one slip at all on that trip. It was amazing! However, one day I took the kids to the Civil War Museum out at Stone Mountain Park. Everything was in glass cases which were kind of tempting to touch. Little Abi has always loved lovely things and there was a display that caught her attention. She wasn't even doing anything wrong, but when she touched the glass case on a corner it sliced her finger open. She had a voice so shrill that echoed through the marbled floor museum I grabbed her hand and pulled her outside just so I could think without the echo, her three siblings in tow. We sat on the steps, and I was thinking, "This needs stitches." I put pressure on it and had a t-shirt to wrap it in to catch the blood. There was a lot of blood.

After only a few seconds of inner panic and a prayer of "Lord, Help!" an elderly man tapped me on the shoulder, As my head turned I saw he was pulling a Band-Aid out of his wallet, "This will do the trick."

His wife nodded, "It will!"

I looked up and forced a desperate, grateful smile through Abi's shrill scream/cry, "Thank you." I took the band-aid quickly and immediately turned to Abi's finger.

"This will help." I said, but I was thinking, "We need a medic, and she may need a transfusion."

I put the Band-Aid on her finger and almost immediately she stopped scream-crying. She sniffled and said, "It doesn't hurt anymore."

That took less than five seconds. I turned to thank the man and his wife, and they were gone. I asked the kids where they went. Mikey said, "They 'missappeared.'"

John, the oldest, said, "They were walking that way," he pointed in the direction of a long straight path, "but they're gone."

Amanda smiled, "I think they were angels." She laughed.

Abi and I agreed.

The bleeding had stopped immediately as well. Two days later when I took the kids to meet up with their parents at Granny K's house we took off the Band-Aid her little finger was totally healed except for the tiniest of white scar tissue to prove that there had been an injury. There was a little dot of blood on the Band-Aid.

Dottie Rambo and Angels with Scrolls

If I've ever been a "fan" of anyone it has to be Dottie Rambo. She was on TBN[25] giving her testimony about her "Angel Room." The short version is that they had purchased a home in Atlanta and were in the process of moving from California. The house was still empty. She had chosen a room in the new home to be her meditation/prayer/inspiration place. One of the young men that were helping them move had arrived before everyone and decided to check out the home. He heard something in Dottie's meditation room. When he tried to go through the door he was knocked back on his heels. He heard voices laughing and singing excitedly. When he finally was able to peek into the room, he saw several "gothic" angels (Dottie's words for large angels with wings) placing scrolls of inspiration for music and melodies around the room excitedly dancing with joy while fulfilling their heavenly assignment. In her testimony, Dottie said," The Lord sends angels to me to carry me to the throne room to give me songs."

---

[25] Video of Dottie Rambo's Angel Room Testimony can be seen here https://www.youtube.com/watch?v=yD2X14HVqdg

That kind of angelic assignment is not unique to Dottie Rambo. She didn't even see the angels herself that day. The young man saw them and Dottie believed the report.

.

What Would You Do If...?

Would you believe it if someone told you that they saw and heard the angels plant God-given inspiration around your studio space? What about if it were in your car or home in general? What if you knew that inspiration for concepts, ideas, witty inventions, or ways to solve knotty problems were planted around you for you to find? Would you feel as frustrated about your circumstances? Or would you center down with the Holy Spirit and start asking him to reveal to you the things that God has prepared for those who love Him? Would you take the time to meditate (fancy word for shut-up and listen) and write down what the Lord is saying to your spirit through the Holy Spirit?

If the Lord prepared things for Dottie, then he has prepared things for you too because you are anointed to fulfill your assignment as much as she was anointed to fulfill her assignment. 1 Corinthians 2:9-10 (AMPC) tells us:

> " ...as the Scripture says, What eye has not seen and ear has not heard and has not entered into the heart of man, [all that] God has prepared (made and keeps ready) for those who love Him [who hold Him in affectionate reverence, promptly obeying Him and gratefully recognizing the benefits He has bestowed]. **Yet to us God has unveiled and revealed them by and through**

> ***His Spirit***, *for the [Holy] Spirit searches diligently, exploring and examining everything, even sounding the profound and bottomless things of God [the divine counsels and things hidden and beyond man's scrutiny]."*
>
> *(1 Corinthians 2:9-10)*

For the longest time I thought that Dottie's experience was one of those "special dispensations of Grace" the old timers used to talk about. That meant Dottie had more clout with God and so she got special treatment. Yet, I have learned through studying the Word that, just like with Dottie, God has prepared things for those who love Him. That includes you and me. Dottie just gives us a little insight about how those preparations take place in the Spirit realm and why it is the Holy Spirit that has to reveal them to us.

Your Assignment is Their Assignment

Ok, this one doesn't seem like rocket science. But would you believe that I'm writing this book because it finally stuck in my mind that I have an assignment? I realized that, along with Holy Spirit, the angels planted inspiration around my life that I've let lay dormant. I've been an award-winning writer since the 4th grade. I wrote a poem about a strawberry blonde cocker spaniel named "Pumpkin" who died and is buried under a willow in a field near grandpa's house. My teacher entered the poem into a competition, and I won first place. I got a medal and a certificate and walked across the stage while people clapped. I was like, "No biggie, I write stuff like that all the time." In 4th, 5th, and 6th grade many students would ask me to sign their yearbooks, not because we were friends but because I would write original poems about them in it.

With all of that, somehow I didn't see writing as a part of God's plan for me. However, he was guiding me and taught me along the way. I was met with discouragement about my writing from every side. Family and friends didn't know how to encourage me with my gift. Sometimes they didn't even see it as a gift but, rather, as a waste of time.

It is a driving necessity for me to find a secluded quiet place to myself ALONE to read and write all sorts of literature and lyrics, finding ways to express myself in words. They called me a hermit or "Belle" from Beauty and the Beast. There were a few encouragers but most didn't see that God had put a talent and desire in me to relay his love, will, and kingdom workings through the written word.

I literally cannot get away from the need to write things from inner inspiration. In the past, I have let the outward nay-sayers steal the true value of my gifting. I just thought I was laying it all up for my kids one day to appreciate that I was more than just a mom. That one day after I'm gone, they might appreciate that I had a soul and deep thoughts. Maybe you can relate to diminishing God's will and purpose for your life because others just don't see it.

Yet, very recently I asked the Lord verbatim (I was in a sassy mood), "God all these preachers be sayin' 'you get into the center of God's will for your life and you'll find your wealthy place!' So I'm here taking care of my disabled parents 24/7, being a good wife to my husband, and a good mom to my kids, and loving on other people's kids and taking care of them, all to help people out. Why am I still struggling? Where is my greater purpose?

The Lord answered me in my spirit very plainly. "Your wealth is in your writing!"

I wrote that down. I made it the wallpaper for my smartphone, my laptop, and my smartwatch. Wealth is not just a money thing, it is a quality of life thing. Suddenly, I'm what millennials call "woke." I have been missing it all this time. The thing that was the easiest for me. The thing I find inspiration for without even trying, the thing I have a passion for. "**That** is what you want me to do, God?! You want me to write?! OK, I'LL DO IT!"

That was my "suddenly." At that moment all my life began to shift to accommodate my gift. Angels began planting miraculous provisions to make room for this gift of writing.

A Little Testimony

I'm writing the bulk of this book on a cruise ship in the Gulf of Mexico. I'm sipping on a diet ginger-ale, sitting on aft deck eleven looking back over the bluest water I've ever seen and tapping out this sentence. Nobody is bugging me. I don't have any meals to cook, any baths to give, any medications to distribute, any questions to answer, any TV to distract, and no WIFI to numb the daily grind with YouTube and what-not. Everything that is not going right back at home is in God's hands. The Angels are on assignment while I'm on assignment. My assignment to write this book for you to encourage you in your daily supernatural life within the Kingdom of God is the angels' assignment too.

You've got to know what a miracle it is for me to be on this ship. My husband has been out of work for the past three months—no income, I didn't have money for a cruise. I would never have planned a cruise without my husband. My confession has been, "The Lord will perfect that which concerns me.[26]" And "He does all things well[27]." I'm here. This was the Lord getting my attention to look for the inspiration. To stop and take time. To allow the angels to do their job and for me to do mine. My assignment is their assignment.

When I finally accepted my assignment from the Lord to be a writer without back-talking him, the angels had to make a way for me to get it done. HAD TO. Their assignment from God is to help me with my assignment from God[28].

There was absolutely no way for me to write this back at home in the time frame that God had put on my heart. I needed some time to think, to write without interruption, to get away from the demands that being a caregiver puts on me. You are reading this because of Supernatural Assistance given to me by God. He inspired my children to buy me a cruise for Mother's Day and blessed them to pay for it. They booked it for the ONLY week this school year I do not have college classes. They didn't even know it.

---

[26] Psalm 138:8

[27] Mark 7:37

[28] Hebrews 1:13 &14

People heard I was getting a break after 5 years of 24/7 caregiving and sent me money to cover expenses I didn't even know existed. One sister sent "fun money" and one sister took off work and came to care for my parents for the 10 days I'll be gone. Even my husband not having employment at the time has been a blessing. The Lord is talking to him and revealing things to him on levels we've never known. This is Supernatural Assistance at its finest.

Let me ask you, What is your assignment from God? Know this: You have a heavenly host available to help you with it, once you've accepted it and focus on it circumstances have to change in your favor. Believe That!

Signs & Wonders

What are they?

A sign is a happening that points you to something bigger that is going to happen, like the Star in the sky was a sign to the wisemen that a King was born in Bethlehem. That was a showy precursor to an upcoming event. Everyone who looked up could see it, but only people looking for its meaning were able to find the event by it.

A wonder is something that makes us say, "hmm..." or wonder how or why something is done. It sets us to thinking or searching for an answer. Like the shepherds watching their flocks by night. First this angel comes in, lighting up the place scaring them and telling them about a baby. Then the whole night sky lights up with a heavenly host praising God. It made them leave their flocks alone in the night to go and find that baby to worship.

When Jesus did miracles of healing it often was a wonder. How can you make a person who didn't have a leg all of a sudden grow a leg? How? We know this happened because the word tells us that Jesus healed the "maimed" not just the lame.

The Wonder of Brother Biddy and the Angels

Do you remember back in the first chapter when I talked about the blind man with no eyes getting his miracle? I mentioned Brother Biddy. He was a strange looking bird of a man with sharp features, skinny as a toothpick, long, gangly body and long gangly fingers. His hair was kind of curly wavy and slicked back in a Beethovenesque style. He played that Hammond B3 with the Leslie speaker with such skill and anointing that he could make it say, "Hallelujah!" That's not an exaggeration, like some guitarists make their guitar talk, he could make the organ say, "Hallelujah."

I was fascinated with the keyboard and anyone who could play a keyboarded instrument. I was glad when mom would sit us on the front row near the organ so I could watch him play.

On more than one occasion as he would worship God while playing the organ, he would become overwhelmed by the Holy Spirit. We would say, "The Spirit hit him." So when the Spirit would "hit" him, first he'd start shouting in tongues, still playing the organ with his eyes closed. He had a whoop that he'd let out, and I knew the place was about to get lit. It was one of those Sundays when the Blind Man received his eyes. That kind of stuff is just what happened on those Brother Biddy-shouting days.

He'd stand up off of the organ seat and be on his toes dancing out the bass notes on the foot board like a holy ghost river-dance and that bass board would thump out a sound that I still listen for when I hear an organist play. It was percussive as well as melodic. If I were to compare it with something today it would be Dub Step music because you could feel it in your chest.

While he was doing that with his feet, his head would be whipping back and forth like a chicken and his coke-bottle glasses would fly off. OOHH Buddy! It's on like a neck bone now! His fingertips would barely be touching the keys, but he would be banging out a song like he was playing for all of heaven, hell, and everything in between to hear it. It was high praise, warfare, and worship coming out of that strange man on the organ.

Then, on very special Sundays, the Holy Ghost and Brother Biddy would take it to the next level. He'd be up on his toes, up on his finger tips and let out a whoop and he would take off dancing a high-step run across the church...BUT THE ORGAN KEPT PLAYING.

Brother Biddy would be on the complete opposite side of the church cutting a rug for Jesus and both keyboards and the foot boards were being played by someone from God's unseen army—an Angel. We kids knew it was going on because we were sitting there watching Brother Biddy because he was oh-so watchable but the adults were so lost in the same high praise, warfare, and worship that had overtaken Brother Biddy, that they were dancing to the music and shouting and lost in God's presence.

I've never seen anyone play like that since but it is a level I strive for. I desire to pour myself out so completely in worship that the Angels must take over a minute while I just lose myself in HIM.

Heavenly Chorus

Worship is a running theme within my family. Just so we're on the same page, no, I'm not talking about the slow songs that people sing with the word "God" in them. Actually, most of them are not even worship. Worship is "extreme submission to and extravagant love of" something or someone. So, worship songs are songs, whether slow or fast, that are sung as an act of extreme submission and extravagant love to God. Kari Jobe's "Revelation Song," and Hillsong's "So Will I" are great examples of modern worship. They speak of loving and adoring God and making his nature our nature, not just thinking about it or singing about it, but actually doing it.

Worship is something that we press into and when we are in a time of worship with music, wonders are always in the atmosphere.

One day, when dad was a new pastor of a small congregation in Neodesha, KS he went into the sanctuary to pray and praise. As he worshiped the Lord there he took out his guitar and turned on his reel to reel recorder (were talking late 60's early 70's here) and he just worshiped until the reel ran out. He ran it back and listened to it. When he started, it was just him but very soon as the worship deepened he was joined by a few voices in harmony and then a choir of voices behind him worshipping God in glorious melodies and harmonies of a heavenly chorus. He took the recording back home and had mom listen to it. He asked her how many voices she heard. "Well, Roland. It sounds like a choir to me."

That choir still shows up every once in a while, when dad starts worshiping. I don't know what opens the heavenly door to bring them into our hearing range, but I believe that they are always worshipping with us. I'll tell you why I believe that in a few chapters when I describe the vision of heaven the Lord gave me.

Glory Clouds

I'm not a hater when it comes to the use of the finest of equipment to create an atmosphere for worship. It is not unscriptural to have real fire that has real smoke in a place to prepare people for God's presence[29]. So don't think I'm knocking all those fog machines out there where people are using their best creative skills to create an atmosphere for the Lord.

However, I've been in Glory Clouds thicker than any fog machine can produce, in an atmosphere of worship that the presence of God was so heavy and palpable that every person in the room was flat on their faces. They are unusual in that each manifestation is a unique manifestation from God, but they are not uncommon where you find true worshipers.

I cannot say that there is a formula that brings a Glory cloud EVERY TIME, but I can tell you that every time there has been a glory cloud there has been three things in practice in a congregation—humility, unity, and prayer.[30] When you get those things working in a church, the manifestations of God's glory are soon to follow. The other thing is to begin to declare the Goodness of God.

In Exodus 33:18, Moses asked God, "Show me your Glory."

---

[29] Exodus 30:8

[30] 2 Chronicles 7:14

The Lord basically told him, "You can't take it, but I'll show you the back side of my glory."

> *And the Lord descended in the cloud, and stood with him there, and proclaimed the name of the Lord. And the Lord passed by before him, and proclaimed, The Lord, The Lord God, merciful and gracious, longsuffering, and abundant in goodness and truth, Keeping mercy for thousands, forgiving iniquity and transgression and sin, and that will by no means clear the guilty; visiting the iniquity of the fathers upon the children, and upon the children's children, unto the third and to the fourth generation*
>
> *(Exodus 34:5-7 KJV)*

We find that the children of Israel recount this instance on days of consecration. King David wrote Psalm 118 as a call and response. He would sing a phrase, and everyone would reply "His mercy endureth forever."

Solomon on the day of dedication of the temple said a prayer then the people sang together, "For the Lord is Good and his Mercy Endures Forever." And fire came down from heaven and consumed the sacrifice. The Glory was so strong that people were laid out before the Lord and could not stand in that Glory.[31]

---

[31] 2 Chronicles 5:13

Mine Eyes Have Seen the Glory!

One such instance of a Glory Cloud was when I was the Worship Minister at a small church in Waycross, Ga. One Sunday morning the we started worshiping the Lord and it was a deep time of worship. I don't remember the exact song we sang but when I opened my eyes the congregation was covered in a haze. I thought I had mascara in my eyes from crying. The pastor got up and stood in the pulpit and said, "I see the Glory Cloud of God in this place today. It is above your head. Some of y'all are in it, some of y'all are repelling it. Humble yourselves and let the Glory overtake you."

It was sad as we watched the cloud stay above most people's heads. But many of us continued to worship and the cloud engulfed us to where all we could whisper was, "You are so good. God you are good."

The act of declaring back to God what he says of himself, "The Lord is Good and His Mercy Endures Forever..." mixed with faith and humility in unity with others after a season of corporate prayer is as close to a formula as you can get for bringing in the Glory clouds.

Glory in a Prayer [bed] Room

At one time of prayer, I was laying out on the floor, praying to God. I wasn't praying for him to do anything, or to be anything more to me than he already was. I just wanted more of him. I felt lost in my skin. Like I didn't fit in the world he'd made. I felt out of my time and place. So my solution to that was to pray and cry and wish and hope that He would answer that prayer one day. Suddenly I felt a heaviness, like a blanket falling on me. I stopped talking, I squeezed my eyes closed as an awesome presence filled the room. I felt like if he spoke that I would die. I didn't want him to leave, but his presence was almost more than I could bear. I didn't understand that he was there to love me—to answer my heart cry. I misinterpreted his presence as his judgment against me and reacted with fear. Looking back at it with better understanding of his Goodness and Mercy, I wished that I had known more about His goodness and lovingkindness.

More Glory in my prayer room

More recently I had been seeking the Lord, I had been having angelic visitations in my prayer times almost daily. I knew it was leading up to something, I knew them coming was a sign pointing to an event. So, one night I closed my eyes and was listening to a song that the Holy Spirit always comes and manifests himself when I play it (Keith Moore's "Great is Our God" from Eagle Mountain's Days of Refreshing: September 16, 2008 (part 5 at about time marker 1:12:00[32]).

That blanket came on me again. The heaviness covered me, and my eyes were closed tight. I recognized Him. He was glad to be there with me. I wish I could tell you that I responded with all the Love he was pouring on me. My spirit was willing, but my flesh was so weak. I said out loud, "I don't want to see you. I think that would freak me out." My sprit was craving his presence, calling out to him but my flesh opened its big mouth. I felt the heaviness lift gently. He was kind, but the feeling of his heavy presence lifted. STUPID FLESH!

---

[32] EMIC Days of Refreshing September 16, 2008, https://www.emic.org/service/2008-days-of-refreshing-part-5/

I thank God for his tenderness with me to not leave me or forsake me even after I did that. I have not had that type of visitation since but I am preparing for it, getting my flesh in "shut-yo-mouth" mode to just praise out of my spirit, "The Lord is Good and His Mercy Endures Forever."

Supernatural Travel: Being "Translated"

My Granny R, Rosa Floye Hughie Robinson (Dad's mom) was a praying woman. She didn't just pray prayers, she went on adventures with God in her prayer time. She would sit in her little rocking chair with her crochet work in her chubby hands and take on the devil and all his little imps. She would have her Dake's Annotated Bible on her lap and a "Shun Di!" On her lips. I promise you when she prayed there were going to be some heavenly hosts moving out on orders in a very few seconds. She was a prayer warrior.

One day she was talking to my mom about her adventures in prayer. She said that once she was compelled to pray for a missionary family she knew. She sat in her chair and began to intercede. As she did she began to see a vision where she stepped off of the last step of an airplane onto the tarmac and her missionary friends were there to meet her. They hugged and they were so happy to see her. They told her how discouraged they were and how they were so glad she'd come to help them.

In her vision, Granny R went with them to their little church building and began to preach and teach the little dark faces that she loved instantly. As she preached, it was as if lights began shining on their faces. She became tired and ended the service. She asked her friends where she was sleeping and that she needed to rest. They gave her a room.

Just as she lay down on the bed she came out of the vision and looked around her. She was disappointed that it had only been a vision, but it had been so real. The next day she felt compelled to pray for the same couple. Again, she was taken in a vision to where they were. They laughed and talked about God and reminisced about the good old days. She prayed for them and encouraged them in the Lord, prophesied, and preached. Then she preached to their little congregation again. The Glory of the Lord began to shine on their faces again as she ministered the word. She ended the service and asked to lie down. Immediately, when she did, she was awake and in her prayer chair.

This same pattern repeated itself for a week. On the last day, she hugged them and stepped her first foot on the steps of the airplane then she was back in her chair.

She told one or two close friends what had transpired. She asked if anyone had gotten a letter from them. This was the era before phones were in every house, there definitely wasn't a phone in the little village where her friends were missionaries. No one had heard from them in months.

Soon Granny R had other prayer assignments to attend to, but that one never left her. The visions were so vivid and real. She wondered what God had done through them or if she should try to go there. It had been a long time since her missionary trip to Jamaica, over twenty years. She didn't feel like, at her age, she could do that any longer. However, she continued to pray for the couple and was excited to hear that their church had blossomed and grown, and they had been able to establish a pastor there and they were coming home.

Granny R was eager to tell them about her visions in her prayer time to perhaps find out their meaning. When she finally saw them they ran to her crying, "Oh, Floyd! We can't thank you enough for coming to us when we were at our lowest! We wanted to quit. When you stepped off of that plane, we were so surprised, we had just said to each other that morning that we were going to quit if God didn't send us help. He sent us you."

Granny R was so shocked that she just told them, "Give God the Glory."

It was a few years after that she finally told them what happened. She tried to tell others but they said she was crazy. She told my mom with the preface, "You may say I'm crazy, but I know this really happened."

Mom believed Granny R was translated. I believed her too... and it has happened to me—twice.

My First Supernatural Trip

I was nine (1979). I had been praying for the underground church of Russian believers. I lay across my bed and cried to God for their safety and for the Lord to send them Sunday school teachers to tell them the stories of Jesus.

I fell asleep. My eyes opened and I was surrounded by a room full of adults. I was telling them the stories of the Apostle Paul, how he went from persecuting Christians to the man who was persecuted for Christ. They especially liked the story about the intercessors praying for Paul in jail and how the angels came and led him out of the jail and to the place where the people were praying for him. I was speaking and understanding perfect Russian. The place we were hiding was a dusty back room and we were huddled around a small kerosene heater. The room was stacked with old wooden church pews and beautifully carved wooden pulpit furniture covered in a deep layer of dust and smelled of mildew. It was dark and I whispered to them by a small shaft of moon light and incandescent shine from the heater that was in the middle of our small group of five or six.

There was a man at the door of the stuffy room. He looked frightened as he listened at the heavy wooden door for the sound of footsteps in the hallway.

They told me to continue. So, I did. I must've told them ten or more stories when the man at the door gave us the alarm, "They're here."

The men wrapped me in a thick tapestry and opened a window. They put me out in the freezing cold night onto a fire escape. When I rolled out of the tapestry I was in my bedroom and still laying on my bed, but my body was ice cold from the Russian winter wind my face felt wet from melting snow. For a while after that, I could still understand Russian. I didn't have anyone to talk to in the language, so I lost the skill.

My Second Trip

I was 27 years old (1997) and hungry for more of God. Inwardly I felt like I was floundering, not reaching my purpose. Outwardly, I was on a fast track to renown and success. I was on the ministry staff of an on-fire church in Jonesboro, GA that was growing and affecting the community for Christ alongside ministers who are making an international mark today. Name-dropping isn't my style, but you'd probably know them if I did.

Something BIG was missing.

One day I had to travel to Waycross, GA on a semi-emergency concerning my grandmother (Mom's mom). It was a four-hour trip for me because I don't make it a habit to drive above the speed limit. Mom was there at the time and so I was glad to go. I felt that I needed to see her because she would understand on a spiritual level without me trying to explain all of the details and I was on a tight schedule. I had to be back in Jonesboro by that night for outreach the following morning.

I drove down I-75 to Tifton with a heaviness on me. This was before cell phones so I was alone and disconnected from distraction. I prayed in tongues and felt like the world was getting heavier and heavier on me. I didn't recognize the feeling or atmosphere in the car. I wondered if it was a part of the Lord that I had never experienced before.

When I arrived at Granny K's (Mom's mom) house, Mom met me at the door, "What's going on?" her voice laced with concern.

"Mom, I can't stay." I told her with not a bit of understanding why, "I am about to have an encounter with God, and I don't understand it."

She knew it was true but the look of concern on her face was one I'd only seen when she was travailing in prayer. I was glad to see it, but it was also a bit disconcerting. She was praying for me, travailing for me.

I did the work I needed to do quickly. I kept telling mom, "I have to go soon. I can't stay."

She helped me get things done so I could. "Do you feel like you are being driven into the wilderness?" She asked. It was a reference to Jesus being driven into the wilderness to pray and fast.

I could only nod.

As soon as our task was finished, I said my goodbyes and had a sense that it may be my last goodbye so I hugged mom tightly and turned to leave. "Take the back way." That was what she called the way through Albany to Interstate 16 east of Macon. She said it before I could turn and told her that was the way I was planning to go. "I am," I replied looking into her eyes.

We hugged again and I got in the car and left.

As I drove up the back way to Albany, GA to hit I-16 to Macon the car was empty except for my prayers. I didn't sense the Spirit of the Lord, my spirit, or any evil spirit. I just drove the very familiar route, same as always. Something shifted in the car. I realized I wasn't on the same route. I was several miles off course to the east when I arrived at I-16. There had been no detours, no recognizable differences in my course but I was about thirty miles east of my usual on-ramp, closer to Savanah than Macon.

When I merged into the midday/early evening traffic I felt something enter the car behind me. I looked in my rearview mirror to see what was back there, convinced I'd see something or someone from the spirit realm, but nothing was there.

I asked the Lord aloud, "What is that?"

His reply was, "That is Death."

I wasn't afraid because it was a familiar presence. I recalled it from a time in Louisiana when I'd gone with a friend to pray for her friend in the hospital. I had prayed with the man but when I stood at his feet I sensed that presence. I asked God, spirit to Spirit (not out loud) if the man was going home, "Yes." Was his reply, "He's coming home to me, it's all right."

So, the spirit I felt in the car with me was not there to frighten, or to do me harm. It was just there because, when Death happens, no one is ever alone, and I knew that death was there for me.

"You are going to go down this highway, a truck is going to cross the median and you're going to die." The Lord stated emphatically. I thought about slowing down or speeding up but there was an understanding in me that it would make no difference as if it were my appointed time.

I felt disappointed and sad for myself, but still no fear. "What will people say about me?" I asked him with the first bit of emotion.

"That it was too soon and that you were too young, and it was a waste."

"It's not enough, Lord," I replied with tears. I thought for a moment about a minister at the church where I was working. He loved

God and people with passion. It was a mystery to me how he could do it. People assumed that I was "In love with him" but that was far from true. I was like a kid watching an artesian blow glass. He didn't judge people, he didn't condemn people, he didn't make people clean up before he presented God to them...he just loved them. I loved God, but I really didn't love people...and I didn't love myself. This was a flaw—a fatal flaw, and I knew it.

"Lord, I want people to say that I Loved!" The tears flowed even deeper now because I was not only seeing how wasteful my life and ministry had been because the one thing that God commanded was that we love, and it was the one thing that no one could really say I ever did. I had been so hurt, so guarded, so distrustful, so judgmental; and love cannot grow and thrive in a fearful heart.

"God, if you let me live, I will spend my life learning to love you and to love others how you love and when I die people will know your love through me." I sobbed with resignation, "If that's not possible, then I commend my spirit into your hands right now."

I heard the Lord say, "Good enough!"

The spirit of Death left the car. Immediately a small white truck, like a Ford Ranger or Nissan Frontier, that was going east as I headed west, jumped the guardrail in front of me crossed the highway at breakneck speed, and without slowing down ran up the hill and hit a tree. To me it looked like the driver's head came through the window unattached from his body.

Immediately, I was at my exit to get to my home in Jonesboro, Tara Boulevard. When I got home, I looked at my watch. It was less than two hours since I'd left Waycross. I called mom and told her where I was. She was amazed. "That's not possible," She gasped. Then her tone changed, "What happened?"

I couldn't talk about it. It was a sacred moment, and I hadn't found words for it. "I can't talk about it right now mom. But I'm ok. I had an encounter with the Lord and I'm already safe at home."

I could hear the relief in her voice, "Thank GOD."

"I love you, mommy," I said from an open place of love in my heart I'd never tapped into for anyone. "I Love You, Linda-Bug." She replied. "When you can talk about it, I want to know."

Since that day, the Lord has held me to that vow of learning to live in the Love of God.

In less than six months the Lord took me out of that place of wonderful people who loved me more than I could understand and placed me in the most uncomfortable places, vulnerable and forced to love beyond my comfort zone. People no longer had to earn my love they only had to need it. And I found out that everyone on the planet **NEEDS** the Unconditional Love of God. I am not perfect in my love walk by anyone's stretch of the imagination, but I am being perfected by it.

Defeated Demons

Then Jesus made a public spectacle of all the powers and principalities of darkness, stripping away from them every weapon and all their spiritual authority and power to accuse us. And by the power of the cross, Jesus led them around as prisoners in a procession of triumph. **He was not their prisoner; they were his!**

Colossians 2:15 (TPT)

Under Our Feet

This section is not to glorify demon powers or to give them place above the one that the Lord put them; and that is below the lowest power in the universe. This chapter will not breed fear, because Jesus Christ defeated all demonic powers including their leader Satan at the cross; Colossians 2:15 says "...making a show of them openly". I like the Passion Translation of Colossians 2:15,

> *Then Jesus made a public spectacle of all the powers and principalities of darkness, stripping away from them every weapon and all their spiritual authority and power to accuse us. And by the power of the cross, Jesus led them around as prisoners in a procession of triumph.* **He was not their prisoner; they were his!**

Doesn't that just put goosebumps on your goosebumps! Rick Renner in his fabulous book entitled "Sparkling Gems" breaks this down even further when he tells us,

> *"He gallantly strode into heaven to celebrate his victory and the defeat of Satan and His forces. As a part of His triumphal process, He flaunted the spoils seized from*

> *the hands of the enemy. Yet the greatest spectacle of all occurred when the enemy himself was openly put on display as bound, disgraced, disabled, defeated, humiliated, and stripped bare..."*
>
> *(Renner, Sparkling Gems, p. 75)*

So, in reading this section you need to keep in mind that this is not a glorification of the powers of darkness but rather a spectacle of a defeated foe in a power struggle for this earthly realm in order to fulfill his lust for power. This power-lust can be seen in Isaiah 14:12-14:

> *How art thou fallen from heaven, O Lucifer, son of the morning! how art thou cut down to the ground, which didst weaken the nations!*
>
> *For thou hast said in thine heart, I will ascend into heaven, I will exalt my throne above the stars of God: I will sit also upon the mount of the congregation, in the sides of the north:*
>
> *I will ascend above the heights of the clouds; I will be like the most High.*
>
> *(Isaiah 14:12-14 KJV)*

In this scripture is the whole answer to why Satan/Lucifer hates mankind so much. We were created in God's image and likeness, with dominion and authority over creation even angels—**even him and his fallen angels.** The very thing he desired to do—ascend on high, exalt his throne above the stars of God, and be like the most High—those things we have achieved by God's creation of mankind and after the fall by Grace through faith in Jesus and what He did on the cross.

Ephesians 2:6-7 in the Amplified Classic Translation tells us:

*And He **[the Father]** raised us up together with Him **[Jesus]** [when we believed], and seated us with Him **[the Father]** in the heavenly places, [because we are] in Christ Jesus, [and He did this] so that in the ages to come He might [clearly] show the immeasurable and unsurpassed riches of His grace in [His] kindness toward us in Christ Jesus [by providing for our redemption].*

(Bolded italics mine, inserted for clarity)

As you can see, we, through no personal effort, work, strategy, or plan of our own have been freely given what Satan and his fallen angels (demons) have been in a spiritual power grab for since before Adam was given his first breath.

Satan thought that he could achieve it by dethroning Adam and placing this "in-the-image-of-God" creature under his fallen, rotten feet. Satan felt he had won when this man had bowed to eat the fruit of the tree of knowledge of good and evil but God already had a plan in place to thwart Satan's efforts. He had a woman... and her seed (Jesus) would bruise the Serpent's (Satan's) head and only get a bruise on His heel for his trouble. HA HA!

An Angry Devil

Do you remember back in the first section on miracles that I told you about the blind man who received his eyes? Well, wherever miracles happen, I've found that demons try to come in and distract from the work of the Lord. They try to stir up fear so that faith in God is squelched. Fear and faith are completely incompatible.

I was that little five-year-old and was sitting by Mom on the front row of the church while Dad preached. Dad had started preaching his message when a blood-curdling scream came from the other side of the church. A man picked up a chair and threw it straight at Dad while this shriek continued. The chair **ricocheted off the air in front of dad** and hit the side door of the sanctuary so hard that the thick wood door dented and splintered. The man screaming began to growl like an animal and my Granny Robinson broke out in tongues (praying in the Holy Ghost). Dad said, "Don't be afraid folks, it's just a demon trying to show out." Then he rebuked the spirit in the man to shut up and sit down. The man sat down but kept growling under his breath.

"If you want this devil to leave you" dad spoke to the man, "I'll cast him out right now and you'll be rid of it for the rest of your life, but if you want to keep it, you have to leave and stop disrupting the flow of the Spirit of God.

The man did not want the spirit to leave him. He felt that it gave him power. So, he stood up, screaming and cussing down the aisle.

Dad called after him, "When you are ready to be free of that demonic power you know how to reach me."

As the man left Dad turned to the congregation, "Let's pray in the Holy Ghost."

All the people began praying in the Spirit and worshiping God until there was no residue of fear left in the church and then he continued his sermon.

A few years later I asked Dad how the chair the demon-possessed man threw missed him. He told me that it must have been an angel shielding and protecting him.

That is my first memory of knowing there was a such thing as demon possession other than the Bible stories about demoniacs, but it would not be my last encounter with the forces of darkness.

She Vomited Slime

In my teens we left the church in Atlanta and eventually wound up on the road as full-time evangelists. We crossed the United States, ministering at churches from seven members to seven thousand. Our mission was to strengthen pastors. In one particular church in Maryland that happened to be a culturally African American church, there was a woman who was an attendant (a lady dressed in white who stood around the other women who were dancing in the spirit to keep them from running into people or things). I could see the darkness behind her eyes but I did not discern that there was anything other than sadness in her life.

As she helped others with compassion the darkness in her grew. The pastor's wife walked over to her and took her hand. "Come on, baby. Let's get you prayed for next."

I was on the piano and less than five feet away from the woman at the altar. The pastor's wife kept the woman's arm as she began shaking her head as if saying "no" but the sounds coming out were otherworldly. It was creepy.

I started playing the chorus "You are my hiding place, you always fill my heart with songs of deliverance whenever I am afraid, I will trust in you!" I still laugh when I think about it.

Thankfully the pastor's wife was not afraid at all as dad walked over to the woman and the demons inside her started screeching and choking her. Dad had a word of knowledge, "You have had murder in your heart, you have been so abused, and murder came into your heart. But the Lord is setting you free and the love of God is healing those things in you right now!"

The demons growled, "She's mine. I'm not going!" The acrid smell of death filled the room and the atmosphere became stagnant and heavy with an intimidating fear.

Dad rebuked the demons and said, "I forbid you to manifest any longer! You shut up and come out of her, IN JESUS' NAME!"

By this time I was pleading the blood, hiding under the shadow of His wings, and hoping songs of deliverance would fill my heart very quickly because I was afraid. Don't judge.

Her face was contorted into the most hateful, evil, violent-filled darkness I had ever seen, she started puking up slime. It looked just like the ectoplasm from "Ghostbusters"—florescent green pouring out of her nose and mouth. The Pastor's wife had a Kleenex—just a regular thin Kleenex—in her hand and grabbed the slime with it and pulled. It drew back. She tugged again and pulled, and it dropped to the floor and it disappeared. I was grossed out, but the fear had left and turned into a strange curiosity. The atmosphere changed from heavy and dark to light and joy.

The woman held her hands up and started praising God. As it turned out, she had a butcher knife she had decided to kill someone after church when she got home. The Pastor's wife went with her to get it and throw it away and helped her move out of the place where she was being so abused.

At that time, I thought that was the weirdest demonic manifestation I would ever see, but it wasn't.

She Vomited Frogs

The strangest was in Grand Isle, Louisiana when we had an evangelistic service where all the churches on the island participated except the Catholic church—but many of their parishioners came.

Again, I was on the piano, and my sister, Brenda, was singing with me at that time. Dad had preached a fiery message about God answering the prayers of the saints and mama's prodigal children would come home.

What we didn't know was the very large woman sitting near the back was the local "bad girl." Dad had a word of knowledge and first spoke generally to the congregation, then zeroed in on her, "I want to say this. This is the Lord. God says, 'You have been hurt, cut, beaten...you keep coming to Jesus but then the people that say they are of God take bets on how long it will be before you fall. They plot to make you fall. The Lord says, 'I love you this day, I did call you, I am calling you, and it was not me. It was NOT ME that hurt you.' Says the Lord.' Come to me and I will set you free and make you a new creation.'"

The atmosphere of darkness in the church was heavy and had a rancid smell like rotting flesh and sewerage and body odor. The woman walked toward the front. As she did dad rebuked the congregation (which was most of the religious people on the island). "Shame on you for your lack of compassion for God's child. I can't believe you took bets and enticed her to fall back into sin rather than encouraging her to stay in the Kingdom. Shame on you all."

When she reached the front of the church, I looked over at my sister who was praying in tongues. Don't laugh, but I pulled out the "You Are My Hiding Place" song again.

Dad spoke to the woman with kindness but authority, "You have been so hurt, but you have hurt others as well. Your home is full of pornography, instruments of witchcraft—voodoo-like things." The woman nodded with her head down. "You are not coming to me; you are coming to Jesus." He spoke gently. The woman looked up at him and her face came through, "I'm coming to Jesus."

She jerked back and the devils began to manifest. Dad took authority over them, "You stop that right now, you are not going to hurt God's precious one and you are not going to spread fear in this place! BE QUIET AND BE STILL!"

As loud as he was in authority with the demons, the opposite was true when he was speaking to the woman, "Darlin' Jesus is going to make you free right now. You just in your spirit bow down to him and then out loud say, "Jesus is Lord."

She said the words and then Dad SCREAMED! "I ADJURE YOU SATAN, IN THE NAME OF THE LORD JESUS CHRIST, WHOSE WE ARE AND WHOM WE SERVE, COME OUT OF HER AND ALL YOUR LITTLE IMPS!" His words were an electric fire in the atmosphere. At that moment several people ran out of the back of the church. Turns out they were some of the men who had bet they could get her to fall back to her old ways in less than two weeks. One was her pimp.

The demons didn't come out screaming, dad had forbidden them to manifest that way, but she puked up big black frogs (they looked like fat bullfrogs) that disappeared into the floor. Not all of them came out as frogs, many of the demons whooshed past my sister and me, out of the window behind me, my hair moved from the breeze and Brenda's skirt was blown to the side as if she were in a gale-force wind.

The woman finally screamed, but it was her—it wasn't a demonic scream, but a grief-filled scream of great sorrow, then she fell—like a dead person—onto the floor.

She lay there a long time and started speaking in tongues. Dad put his hand on her head, "You religious spirit! Come out!" He knew by discerning spirits that it was not the Holy Spirit speaking through her. It came out and her body jerked. The demonic spirit whooshed past Brenda and me and smelled of burnt eggs (sulfur). She lay there sobbing, "They're gone. I'm free."

When her two daughters helped her to her feet—they were teenagers about 16 and 18— the woman's clothes were hanging off of her. She had gone from a large woman to petite in less than 5 minutes. She had to hold her clothes on to keep them from falling to the floor. Her physical body had shrunk. At first, she looked like she was about 5'1" and 240 pounds, and when it was finished, she looked like she weighed 180.

Dad looked at her, "People are still going to try to make you fall. You are going to need the real Holy Ghost, and you are going to need to clean out your home."

"I want the Holy Ghost!" She smiled the brightest smile, and her daughters who were still holding her up wept, "Me too." The three of them were filled with the Holy Spirit and that night with the help of the preacher's wife held a Holy Ghost bonfire at their home, burning all the voodoo, fortune-telling, pornography, and witchcraft-inspired paraphernalia.

She came back the next night and I didn't recognize her at all. She was even smaller than before. She and her daughter's countenance glowed. She testified, "I have the Holy Ghost now, I know what real power is. I forgive everyone that used and abused me. Instead of cursing you with voodoo, I am going to pray for you."

It turns out that she had a reputation for putting curses on people that would come to pass. She would send "shadow people" out to the people she cursed with an assignment to do them harm or kill them.

God is a reacher! He will reach anyone where they are to deliver them from the powers of darkness. Someone has to preach deliverance. Someone has to testify to the power of God. Read and study 2 Timothy to ground yourselves that the supernatural power of God is manifest in godly people. You are called to walk in the power of God in this day and hour.

The Devil Has Limits

Demonic manifestations in the form of people vomiting out slime, frogs, snakes, mice, and other creatures isn't a new or unique phenomenon. Indonesian Revivalist, Mel Tari, chronicles many such instances in his books, "Like a Mighty Wind" and "The Gentle Breeze of Jesus." The late Lester Sumrall, a powerful missionary, evangelist, and founder of the Family Broadcasting Network and LESEA International, wrote extensively about his experiences with demonic forces where that would manifest, attack people, move objects, and try to enforce their rule of fear on people. There **never was one time** when demons were not subject to the Authority of the Name of Jesus spoken by a submitted and humble child of God.

> *"Between the beginning of your spiritual life and the end of your life, the devil tries to discourage you; he tries to beat you down; he tries to get you to stop; he tries to get you to go back. The devil does everything he can to keep you off God's target. If you will determine from the beginning that you are going to live on target with God, there are not enough devils to keep you off target!"*
>
> *(Lester Sumrall)*

Brenda and the Fortuneteller

To put it mildly, my sister, Brenda Moody, ain't afraid of no devil. While I was over there playing, "You are My Hiding Place" she was praying in tongues and warrior mode. She has the gift of discerning spirits and is very accurate and can see them coming a mile away, possession, oppression, operating in sowing discord and strife, depression...She just *knows* when it is a demonic force.

In 1997 The Lord had her fasting. It was a weird fast because she mostly ate peaches and water, every morning she would have 8oz of milk, but it was peaches and water for weeks! I asked her if she had an eating disorder several times, but she would assure me that it was a Holy fast. I didn't understand it fully, so I just prayed for her and watched from the sidelines.

I thank God I was there to see the reason for her fast. It was about thirty days into it when she felt the Lord tell her to go to McDonald's on Moreland Ave. (we lived near downtown Atlanta at that time). We got in her teal Ford Festiva and she drove.

As we went the backroads from our place of work towards McDonald's Brenda started praying in the Holy Ghost aggressively. I felt the anointing in it, but she drives fast when she is praying that way so I was also white-knuckling the handle that dangled from the ceiling of the car above the window.

"I am through with the devil running and ruining people's lives. God has a movie waiting to happen. People are hungry for the supernatural that they are looking for it anywhere they can find it!" She was preaching at me and then let out a line of tongues in the Holy Ghost.

When we turned into the drive-thru at McDonald's she pointed to the fortune teller's house that sat on a little hill next door to it. It had a big red palm reading sign and horoscope symbols painted on it. Brenda pointed to it and said, "You get the day off. No fortune-telling today! Woman, you are going to know that God has visited you today!" She was kind of laughing when she said it.

A calm came to her and then she said, "I want fries and a double cheeseburger!"

I'm sitting there blinking and catching my breath. Her change in demeanor would give most people spiritual whiplash, it was so sudden and different.

I asked her if her fast was over, and she shrugged, "Looks like it."

I told her to order my usual, "The All-American Meal with a Dr. Pepper." In the 90's an All-American Meal was a happy meal for adults. A regular cheeseburger, regular fries, small drink, and no toy.)

We had almost made it to the ordering speaker when someone banged on our window. Brenda and I both jumped.

"Where are they?! Where did they go?! What did you do?!" The rail-thin woman in cornrow braids and dark black irises on yellowed eyeballs looked very afraid, she was wearing a red slip and nothing else. "They are gone! Where are they?" She went to the drive-thru window and banged on it, "They are gone! They left me! They are gone!"

The person at the drive-thru opened the window and talked to her. She appeared to be panicked and disoriented. She ran down the street calling for "them."

When we got to the window, the person at the drive-thru turned out to be the daughter of the woman running down the street. Brenda asked her if the woman was all right.

"My mom is the fortuneteller from up there," she pointed toward the house, "All her friends flew out of the house screaming and she says there's an angel with a flaming sword on her porch that says they can't come back." There was fear in her eyes. "She has always had those friends. They are gone and she's scared. I don't know what's going on!"

Brenda witnessed to her, "All of that is a misuse of your mother's gifting and calling. It has brought nothing but sorrow to her and your family. That angel is there to help you not harm you." She took her hand as she passed her the money, "I prophesy a new season in your family's life. I break the power of early death off you. You will live and not die." Then she added, "Can I get some extra ketchup in my bag please?" We had almost half a bag of nothing but ketchup packets when we received our order from the next window.

The palm reader's sign came down less than a week later and the house was empty. A month or so later the house and hill had been razed to the same level as the McDonald's and another fast-food restaurant soon went up on the property.

I Hope You Are Noticing a Trend

Do you see the trend here? That every time there is a meeting of light and darkness, the spirits of darkness are subject to the authority of Jesus' Name?

The Devil and his imps are powerless when confronted with a **humble, submitted,** child of God standing in their authority as a believer.

Three books I believe every Christian should read are John A. Macmillan's "The Authority of the Believer", Kenneth W. Hagin's "The Believer's Authority", and Rev. Owen Murphy's "When God Stepped Down from Heaven." The reason I say this is that they teach Believers in Christ to walk in their God-given place of authority over the enemy in humility towards God; prayer becomes a dynamic force rather than a begging session.

No one who has called on the name of the Lord should be afraid of the devil.

Fear Hath Torment—Until Mama Gets the Broom!

Demonic powers like to harass the people of God. Just like angels are there to bless, help, and assist, demonic forces are there trying to steal, kill, and destroy! Their weapons are not new, not even stealthy or sophisticated. The Bible gives us the demonic ranks in Ephesians 6:12:

> "For we wrestle not against flesh and blood, but against principalities, against powers, against the rulers of the darkness of this world, against spiritual wickedness in high places." (KJV)

The Amplified Bible is even clearer in its description:

> "For we are not wrestling with flesh and blood [contending only with physical opponents], but against the despotisms, against the powers, against [the master spirits who are] the world rulers of this present darkness,

> *against the spirit forces of wickedness in the heavenly (supernatural) sphere." (AMPC)*[33]

When we read this in the Word we are not supposed to react with fear. Fear is for the unknown. Fear is for when you don't know what you are facing, and you don't know what to do. The word of the Lord says in 2 Timothy 1:7:

> *"For God did not give us a spirit of timidity (of cowardice, of craven and **cringing** and **fawning fear**), but [He has given us a spirit] of power and of love and of calm and well-balanced mind and discipline and self-control." (AMPC)*

This is the scripture that my mom displayed on countless occasions. Demons don't always manifest in a physical form, but they come in to a home, or are sent into a home, or are invited into a home, and someone has to take authority over them and tell them where to go.

This was the case when we lived in Neodesha, KS, and demonic activity kept happening in our home. Objects would move, shadow creatures would walk across the room in the darkness, all kinds of ghostly apparitions would appear and torment us at night. They would whisper

---

[33] <u>Amplified Bible, Classic Edition</u> (AMPC) Copyright © 1954, 1958, 1962, 1964, 1965, 1987 by <u>The Lockman Foundation</u>

our names and touch or grab us. Fear of that would overtake me and I would not even be able to scream or breathe.

One night as she prayed while doing the dishes, mom recognized there was a demonic presence in the house. She started laughing and yelled out loud, "AH HA! You're Caught!" She picked up her broom. She went upstairs and started sweeping and talking in tongues. I don't have a theology about this, it is just what happened. She declared as she swept, "You can't stay, you get out of my house!" She swung that broom like she was shooing a cat or a rat out of the house, she wasn't dusting the floor. She went from room to room aggressively swinging the broom toward the exit and shouting, "Get out of my house, in the Name of Jesus. The Blood of Jesus is on the windows and doorposts of this home!" She opened the front door and shouted, "Get out of this house and stay out! In Jesus' Name!"

We followed her through the house watching her like she was crazy but when she slung the last swing at the threshold of the door her broom hit an invisible entity with a thud and the bristles of the broom bent backward. It let out an audible pain-filled scream. Mom yelled out to the front yard, "The Angel of the Lord encamps round those who fear Him! Angel, do your job and keep the devil out of this house!"

We all looked at each other and started laughing an awkward, "*what the heck just happened here?*" kind of laugh. We never had another ghostly manifestation at that house again. That's not to say that those things never happened again in our lives, but when they did, we couldn't say we didn't know what to do.

Mama and the KKK

My mom was a spiritual force. To look at her she just looks like a little southern lady with no sharp edges at all. She laughs easily and finds joy in things that most people see as drudgery, like laundry and dishes. Don't let that diminutive, joy-filled facade fool you. The devil was always very afraid of my mom. VERY AFRAID!

My parents never allowed racism and prejudice in our home. We were taught to appreciate cultures and love people. This was not a popular opinion to have in the 1970s in Atlanta, GA. Atlanta was barely a decade out of desegregation, and the wounds of racism were still raw. The KKK was still out in full force burning crosses and lynching people.

Because my parents pastored a non-denominational, racially inclusive church, and dared to preach that on radio and television, our family became a target.

One night we were all headed to bed in our home on Vernon Ave. and we heard a clamor outside. Our front door was a big oval of beveled glass, and we could all see the hooded men out on the lawn with torches screaming profanities and calling us n***er lovers. Dad happened to be out of town at a preaching engagement.

Mom opened the door, and we all went out behind her.

"You put that out right now!" she demanded. "You are scaring the children! I said you put that out right now!"

The mob went silent.

"I know you heard me! Take that hose, "she pointed at the hose still plugged into the spigot from us kids playing that afternoon, "and put that out and go home right now! In the Name of Jesus!

One of the Klansmen decided to be brave and yell out profanity at Mom. The Holy Spirit of discernment hit her, and she started calling them out by name, "I'm in a prayer group with your mother! Does she know what you're doing out here tonight? She will get a phone call from me in the morning!" She told one of them to go back to his mistress and called her name, which was apparently the wife of one of the other men in the white sheets. Confusion rained down on them and the one with all the red patches on his sheet picked up the hose and put out the fire, they pushed it down and then put it back into the back of one of their trucks. They all slithered back into their vehicles in silence and drove away.

We were never harassed by the KKK again. Although, we had similar experiences with threats being called in on the phone. My parents would always handle them the same way, taking authority over the demon trying to intimidate through fear and rebuke them in the name of Jesus. Nothing ever came of the threats, and we didn't live in the fear of them AND YOU SHOULDN'T EITHER!

Dreams & Visions

Dreams and Visions are For Today

God has **not stopped** speaking to humanity through dreams and visions. Although sometimes modern theology will dismiss them, God is still connecting to people through the subconscious mind. This often takes place when we are asleep and there are fewer distractions. The thing is, that you don't even have to be a Christian or believer for the Lord to speak to you through a dream or vision. They are his tools to influence humanity. Although there are many instances of the Lord speaking through dreams and visions to leaders of nations, armies, people groups, etc., he does not limit Himself to the "mighty" but also "normal" people like you and me—moms, dads, businesspeople, teens, youth and even toddlers. Remember that I was just 9 years old when the Lord translated me to Russia through a vision.

Open your heart and know that God wants to speak to you and through you when he speaks through dreams and visions. He is setting you up for success. He is being a lamp to your feet and a light to your path. He is showing you your purpose. He is giving you answers to the knotty problems[34] of your life.

---

[34] Daniel 5:12 <u>Amplified Bible, Classic Edition</u> (AMPC) Copyright © 1954, 1958, 1962, 1964, 1965, 1987 by <u>The Lockman Foundation</u>

The problem with dismissing dreams and visions is that it cuts off a very real communication avenue with God.

The Bible has at least 21 instances of people having prophetic dreams, and over 30 documented visions. In the Old Testament and New, they were considered one of God's main modes of communication to his leaders, ministers, and lay people including Abraham, Jacob, Saul, David, Joseph: the husband of Mary the mother of Jesus, Peter: Christ's Disciple, Paul: The Apostle, and John: The Revelator to name a few.

My First Dream

I had to be around 7 years old when I had a dream that I went to a church with my Dad. That would not have been an unusual occurrence. It wasn't unusual that we would go to visit other churches. As a Ministry Family with Dad a sought-after speaker, we spent most days in church or bible classes of one sort on another. What *was* unusual in the dream was for Dad to take one child with him...or any child unless Mom was along. But in the dream, it was just him and me.

In the dream, we walked up the cement stairs covered in Astro-turf to the double doors entry. They were held open by smiling ushers who welcomed us to a wood panel foyer with a big fresh yellow flower arrangement on a table to the right. There was a big picture window that had the mother's nursing room behind a blue curtain. We were greeted by the pastor. The usher's opened the double doors to the sanctuary and the place was bright with yellow decor. They had beautiful chandeliers of sparkling filigree gold (probably brass) and the lights were in the shape of candles. On the light wood-paneled walls, about every two pews, there was an insert tall thin window to the outside, five on each wall. The carpet was a deep dove gray and rather plush. Someone touched my shoulder and guided me downstairs taking me through each classroom, into the restrooms and back out, then into the fellowship hall where there was a pot-luck meal laid out and women buzzing around it cheerfully placing spoons in various casseroles and taking knives to cakes. That was interesting to me because they cut the cake in half and then cut straight "bread slices" into the first cut rather than cutting wedges. I'd never seen a cake cut that way before. In my young mind I put it into the category of a real experience because it was so real, I smelled the food, the new carpet smell, and I felt the carpet give way under my feet because it had such thick padding. The pews smelled new when we bowed to pray at them. Old pews smell like...well... pew! Everything was so vivid I thought it had been an actual experience.

It wasn't until I was about twelve that my dad asked if anyone wanted to go with him to a church that was having a Revival. I was the only one who said yes. There was no GPS back then and we couldn't find the church, it was in a rural town.

Dad—in another strange twist to this testimony—stopped at a convenience store to ask for directions. He'd never done that before. The man in the car at the gas pump laughed out loud and said, "It is a hard place to find. I'm the mailman, I'll get you there. Dad shouted hallelujahs and told me that it was a sign from the Lord to have that man there at that moment to take us to the church.

It was a winding way of twists and turns, but we finally made it and I looked up at the church seeing the astroturf-covered steps. I said to myself, "I remember coming here before." I picked up my Bible, walking in behind Dad through the double doors into the foyer. There were the yellow flowers and the big picture window. The pastor grabbed Dad's hand, greeting him excitedly.

The pastor acknowledged me brightly, "Hey, sweetie. So glad you came." The usher opened the doors to the sanctuary for us to follow the pastor inside. The lushly padded grey carpet gave way under my feet. Everything was just as I remembered it. We followed him halfway down the aisle when I pulled my dad's sleeve cuff, "I need to go to the ladies' room before service." I whispered. It had been a long trip to get there.

The pastor turned and pointed "Let me tell you where they are."

"I know where they are." I interrupted, "I've been here before." The pastor and dad laughed outright.

"Darlin'," the pastor patronized me, "there's no way you've been here before." He patted my shoulder.

"Yes, I have" I insisted, "The restrooms are downstairs next to the classrooms between the fellowship hall and the door to the kitchen. The restrooms are done in wood paneling and the ladies' room has two stalls, two sinks, and a mirror on the back of the door."

The pastor's patronizing gaze faded to perplexity. Dad patted my shoulder, "Linda, they only just finished this building. This is their dedication Revival. You have never been here before because it is new."

The pastor stopped dad, "Now, Brother Robinson, she may have been here in the Spirit, because she just described the downstairs to a T." He said with his face a little pale and taking a step back from me almost reverently, "What else did you see when you were here."

I felt awkward telling him about the cakes and the casseroles in the fellowship hall and the decor in the classrooms, but everything was 100% accurate but the thing that impressed him the most was when I told him about kneeling to pray at the pews and them smelling new. They had reupholstered the pews as a last-minute decision to match the new carpet and because the intercessors said they "smelled like butt."

My Vision of Heaven

This chapter is very hard for me to write. It comes from a very tender place in me. It's not only a tender place for me but for my sister, Brenda, and Mom. I'm sharing this with permission and prayerfully.

It was Mother's Day exactly one year after my sister, Brenda, had miscarried. The loss of that baby was made harder by it being the second one she had placed in heaven. The grief was still very raw. I have never experienced a miscarriage so I could not begin to imagine the life-ache.

I was standing in front of my mirror after talking to Brenda on the phone, both of us getting ready for Mother's Day at church. I asked God to comfort my sister and somehow let her know that everything was fine. Suddenly, the mirror in front of me disappeared and I was having an open vision. I was in heaven and hearing the voice of Brenda's first child who had been in heaven for almost 12 years speak to me as if dictating a letter to his mom. The following are excerpts from that vision that I wrote down immediately after it happened.

Brenda, I have to write this to you and tell you what happened after we hung up from talking today.

My house was filled with the tangible presence of God as the night before Mackenzie (my daughter) had watched the DVD "Close Encounters of the God Kind" By Jesse Duplantis. In it, he recounts a visit to Heaven. Every time I watch it or it is watched in my home it is as if the veil between Heaven and Earth is so thin and Heaven becomes as real as the chair I am sitting on now.

I stood in front of the mirror applying my makeup and recalled the Phone conversation that you [Brenda] and I had about how Mother's Day is a year since the baby moved to heaven and your emotions were sensitive about it. In my spirit, I said to God, "What can I do for Brenda? How can I help?" God opened my mind and the eyes of my spirit. And it was as if the child that you miscarried 12 years ago was talking to me to give me a message to you. As if I was the secretary to write this letter to you for him.

I was not necromancing. I was not calling on the spirits of the dead to speak to me. I was putting on my makeup when, like the Apostle, Paul talked about in 2 Corinthians 2:7, whether in the body or out I am uncertain, but the Lord pulled back the veil for just a moment to allow me to see into and hear from the heavenly realm.

This is that letter:

> "Dear Mom,
>
> I know I'm the last person you expected to hear from today, but I know how your heart is yearning to know how things are going here. Well, I wanted to let you know that the baby is here and is doing fine! He arrived in the hand of Jesus— he was so tiny that he fit in the palm of Jesus' hand. Jesus gave him to Father Abraham. You see, Father Abraham is honored to meet and welcome every one of his children first. Then we heard the buzz across heaven that a baby was coming to our house. I was excited to meet my baby brother. Abraham brought him and laid him in MomMom's hands.

> *"She loves the babies. He told us his name is Michael and we call him Michael Alon (Alon means Oak) because he's going to be so tall. He has your blue eyes but is built like Dad."*

As I read this to Brenda over the phone, she was stoic, she didn't believe me until I said the baby's name because she had named the baby Michael in her heart and never told anyone. She began to weep and couldn't let me continue for several minutes.

The letter continued:

> *"I say our house because we live with MomMom and DadDad. We have five uncles here, and lots of cousins.."*

Mom had suffered five miscarriages, at this time in my life I only knew about three of them but when I asked her about it, she confirmed that there were five. I saw them only in opaque shadow, but I saw my brother and his ex-wife's son. He was in his twenties I saw a girl that looked like my niece, Abi, from my sister Paula, whom they called Elizabeth "Peanut" and two children in their teens that belonged to my other siblings, but I was not introduced to them nor given a sense of their names. (I would see Peanut again in a vision after Mom passed away coming to sit with her on a sofa as we talked about Dad going home to heaven.) As Michael would speak I would see what he was describing. MomMom's house with a big arbor over the front gate covered in flowers, in a gingerbread type home that was filled with the smell of something hearty cooking. The yard was lush and green and full of flowers.

"Mom, the nursery was just like you and Dad would have done it yourselves. Yellow--the pretty kind—and lots of lambs and music.

"You know that God lets us hear you sing? It fills up our house when you worship, just like it fills up your house.

"MomMom sews clothes for Me and Michael, (This is Matthew, by the way.) I think the knee pants look silly but they work because Michael is the size of a 6-month-old and just learning how to crawl.

"Granny Robinson gives the best squishy hugs and her house has lots of azaleas, and roses and a dogwood tree that is great fun to climb. I like soccer and have lots of friends at school, by-the-way.

"GiGi [Granny K, my mom's mother but the great grandkids called her Gigi] knows a lot about God..."

[I was taken to her house. It was in the style of a 1920s art deco home with a large sun porch where she had a studio set up to paint.]

"Granny Robinson tells about all the cool things God has done for her and a lot of testimonies...

"...all of us take turns loving up on Michael. Pap Robinson and Granddaddy Kenney like to take turns "dandling" him (ride a little horsy), and he just laughs and laughs.

"You remember the Angel from MomMom's story about the hobo and the beans, He visits us. He is your Guardian angel now. So, he lets us know that you guys are doing good.

> *"I just wanted you not to think that Michael nor I are waiting up here in heaven, lonely and surrounded by angels all day long waiting for some long day away to see you. We are with the family. We eat, play, and work together. We live NOW. We are not waiting to live or didn't get a chance to live. You and us are not even that far apart. You worship our Father [God] and He loves us and lets us be a part of that. When we hear you sing worship, we join in.*
>
> *"We've never known hunger, pain, or fear. But there is a desire—I guess you would call it "hunger" to see you and Dad up close and personal, and our Brother and Sister that are there with you. And everyone keeps telling me that that time is sooner than we think.*
>
> *"With Love from Heaven*
>
> *"Matthew*

I can't speak for Brenda; I can only speak for myself when I say that this was life-changing. I asked God why he didn't tell Brenda this directly. He said that she wouldn't have believed it because of her grief. She would have thought it was her mind playing tricks on her and dismissed it.

He used me to tell Brenda another message from heaven for the same reason very recently—when Mom passed. That is another chapter a bit later in this section.

The Move is On

In Joseph's dreams in Genesis 37:7 & 9, God used symbolism to get tell Joseph his future.

7 "We were out in the field, tying up bundles of grain. Suddenly my bundle stood up, and your bundles all gathered around and bowed low before mine!" (NLT)

9 Soon Joseph had another dream, and again he told his brothers about it. "Listen, I have had another dream," he said. "The sun, moon, and eleven stars bowed low before me!" (NLT)

He told his brothers and they assumed correctly that he was saying that they would wind up bowing down to him.

Again, in Genesis 40:9-18 God used symbolism of wine and bread in the dreams of Pharaoh's cup-bearer and the baker who were in prison with Joseph that he was able to interpret. Which leads to the cup-bearer remembering Joseph when Pharaoh had a disturbing dream full of symbolism-- sheaves and cattle that told of coming 7 years of plenty, and 7 years of famine. This opened the door of opportunity for Joseph to rise to the second in command in all of Egypt and ultimately his brothers coming and bowing down at his feet just like he had seen in his own dreams.

This is the main example of the Lord speaking to men and women in dreams. There are 87 examples in the Bible, Old and New Testaments. I'll let you take the time to explore them all. The Symbolism in these dreams is important.

In my personal life, when the Lord is warning me of troubles coming, I dream about alligators. I have lived in the South Georgia swamp lands of the Okefenokee, and on the edge of the Florida Everglades. Gators are trouble. So, when God wanted to warn me in a dream, he used that particular symbol.

Another symbol he uses for me is tornadoes. Black tornadoes mean bad changes coming suddenly. White tornadoes mean good changes coming suddenly. Tornadoes are always a symbol of sudden change in my prophetic dreams.

Similarly, in my dreams, Snakes are **ALWAYS** symbolic of lies or lying people.

These symbols are strong and when they show up in my dreams, I know to pay attention to the things around me and what is going on because God is trying to get my attention and give me a heads up.

Like I said earlier, the Lord uses dreams to prepare us for things that are coming or are happening now—to reveal hidden things and solve knotty problems.

Up In Their Business

I had one dream about the leadership of a church all washing windows, but one person was jumping in and out of the windows as people tried to wash them and not tending her own window. Her kid came to me crying and said, "Divorce." I just hugged him. I looked outside of the windows and there were alligators, inside were snakes.

When I told her and her husband the dream, before I knew what was happening behind the scenes, he cried and she pretended that it wasn't happening. It made me think that I'd gotten it wrong, she was so adamant. But less than a week later someone spilled the tea all over social media. In a small town, that is the same as going viral.

It turned out that the woman in my dream had started hanging out with her girlfriends from high school—party friends— and was having an adulterous affair in real life and had started taking drugs. She and her husband divorced in less than a year. She was dead in less than four. It destroyed the church. Her children are still dealing with the aftermath of losing their mom so young—the youngest was 18mos. But the Lord was faithful to warn and give a chance for change.

Think a moment of the symbolism in that dream. She was in and out. When she was out, she was in trouble. When she was in, she was lying. It was very clear to me. I didn't have to know specifics to know that the Lord was speaking to me and telling me to intercede for this family.

A week before this lady died the Lord gave me a disturbing dream of a dark tornado back in the town where she and her family lived. My parents lived there as well. When I awoke and was writing the dream, the Lord spoke to my spirit and asked me, "Would you still trust in my love and mercy even if you received bad news from back home?" Immediately I thought he was warning me that one of my parents was going to pass away. I cried and told him I would trust his love and mercy. He brought the song to my spirit that Sis. Mary Green had sung when Sam looked at her and said, "uv, mama."

The love of God is greater far

Than tongue or pen could ever tell

It reaches to the highest star

And reaches to the lowest hell

The guilty pair, bowed down with care

God gave His Son to win

His erring child He reconciled

And pardoned from his sin

(Fredrick Martin Lehman, 1868)

When the phone call came from a mutual friend that she had died in a car wreck I fell beside my bed weeping. I could not see how this could be her end, without any chance of redemption. Then the Lord reminded me of the dream and the song that I had written down in my journal. I turned to the page and read it out loud to my husband. We knew from then on, that somehow God had reconciled this hurt child to him, and she was in heaven. God's ways are high and there are mysteries that we will only know when we get to heaven—but he will reveal things to us to give us peace if we give him time to speak and we listen—heed—his voice.

Changes Coming from the West

Around the same time of the window dream, the Lord gave me another dream. I was standing on an overpass looking out of town toward the West. Out of a bright white cloud came down three tornadoes. Two were bright white, one was gray. I was wondering what was happening over there. It was way down the highway out of town. I started yelling and warning people of the intertwined tornadoes, but everyone was too busy getting ready for Thanksgiving to listen. Suddenly I was at my house and my oldest sister, Paula, was filling my freezer with turkeys and lots of food. When I looked up from the freezer the house was full of her things. I was confused. Why are you putting everything you have in my house?

When I woke up, I didn't understand but I wrote it down anyway.

Around thanksgiving, my husband received a promotion that moved us from Georgia to Texas. Paula and her husband moved her family to Guam to be missionaries and start a school. She moved all of her things into our house where Mom and Dad still would be living, and flew to California before leaving for Guam. The gray tornado was a symbol of something that I have been asked not to share because of the pain it still causes family members, but needless to say it was a foreshadowing of darker things to come and it took several family members in a geographically western direction.

Are you starting to see how God used symbolism in my dreams to tell me of things to come?

Have you had dreams like this but let them go by the wayside only to get a sense of Deja vu when things start changing. What is something that God uses as symbols in your dreams to speak to you?

Another Dream and Vision of Heaven

My parents passed away. Earlier in the book I told you that I have been my parents' caregiver…at the time of writing this chapter it is 2021 and I have placed both parents in the arms of Jesus. Mom transitioned to heaven on January 21, 2021. Dad followed her on April 8th of this same year.

Mom going to heaven was not on my to do list. We had come through the 2020 pandemic with no Covid-19 coming nigh our dwelling. But she fell, broke her ankle, and hit her head on December 22nd and that was the beginning of her rapid decline. There is much about her death that is painful for me to talk about now. It sent me into a deep grief that I had never known. The day before she broke her ankle she told me, "No matter what happens, FINISH THE BOOK!" I was like, "Mom! Nothing could ever make me stop finishing the book. I know it's my assignment."

She prophesied to me, "'My people need to know that I am the God of miracles, STILL!!' Says the Lord, 'My people are destroyed for lack of vision. They need to see me doing miracles in this hour, in this time. Miracles for the moms that don't know where they will turn for their next meal. Miracles for the dads who will have to make a stand against demonic forces in their homes. Miracles for the children who will have been raised without an understanding of how to have faith for miracles. I am moving in my power in this hour' says God, 'I am shaking everything that can be shaken. You will be shaken.'"

I didn't like the sound of the "You will be shaken" part but I assured her I would continue to write and, yes, finish the book. I confess, I have been a struggle.

By December 28 she was in a rehabilitation facility. We were in daily contact but were never allowed to see her. By January 8, she had been diagnosed with Covid-19 she contracted while in the rehab center. She was asymptomatic, so she never had a fever, cough, or any Covid-related symptom. She was doing great, and her ankle was healing well. She was one day away from her leaving the quarantine part of the center when she lost conscientiousness unexpectedly and started having grand-maul seizures. She never regained full consciousness.

ANGRY

"Angry" is an understatement. "Enraged with the fire of a thousand hells" would just about scratch the surface. How could God allow all of this to happen?! How could he let her suffer like that?! How could the miracles that he was so intent on me writing about not be applied to Mom for her healing?! I called foul-- with ANGER!

I know some of you are judging me here, but I am going to be honest...if I didn't have people relying on me, I would have found a bottle of whiskey and crawled into it. I dreamed about just getting drunk and not having to deal with all the pain from losing my beautiful Mom—my precious, kind, loving, believing in me, Mom. She was my daily dose of joy. I loved having her and Dad in my home. I'm weeping as I write this. I still miss them so much.

A "Prophetic" Dream

I was barely asleep a few nights after she passed and I was crying so hard, tears were filling my ears. I felt my spirit begin to lift—not out of my body, but beyond the grief and to a Spiritual place. I was having a dream/vision. In it, I was at the hospital where my mom had been taken. Although I was dreaming, the hospital was the actual hospital in Norman, Oklahoma I have been to many times with my parents and to visit others.

I knew she had already gone to heaven, so I wondered why I was there. I turned to find a place to sit when I saw a big black sofa. Mom was sitting on it. There was a large coffee table between us that blocked me from getting to her to touch her, but I said, "Mom!" And she smiled back and me, patting the sofa for me to sit. Some other people came running down the hallway that leads to the patients' rooms and jumped on the sofa between my mom and me, one of them was Peanut! I knew her from my vision of Heaven about my sister, Brenda's baby. There were two other people I didn't recognize but I knew they were related to me somehow. They were family members that mom called, "used-ta-bes." I asked her, "What's a used-ta-be?" She replied in a saucy, jovial tone, "Well, heaven is not like earth because we are all family. So, I've been up here visiting with the people that used-ta-be my aunts and uncles and family on earth."

She was sitting there with a completely healed body. I had forgotten what her face looked like without grimacing in pain. She had been in pain for years but now she looked beautiful, young, and happy—which kind of made me angrier because I wanted her to miss me more like I missed her (I have a petty side).

We talked about the "used-ta-bes" for a while and my attitude softened. I enjoyed talking to her. Then her face took on a very serious expression. She told me that we had made the right decision to put a DNR in place and let her go. She said she would not have been the same after the seizures and that she had already left her body before the ventilator was removed. She told me to tell my sister, Brenda, that she had done the right things regarding the preparation of her body. Because of Covid-19 restrictions we were not able to have a family viewing nor a funeral. We had a 15-minute window with which to prepare the body and say our goodbyes and that with dressing and doing her makeup. *(Side note: Brenda and her husband, Greg, were tasked with the body identification and preparation. No one else could attend. Mom's body had not been properly refrigerated. Brenda and her husband Greg were the only ones to view Mom's body to verify it and to sign the paperwork for her cremation. Mom wanted Brenda to know that she had made the right choices, even though they were different than what we had always planned.)*

I don't remember standing up, but I found myself standing facing the hallway where the people had come from. I saw dad standing on the threshold between the waiting room and the hallway. I asked him, "Are you coming or going?" He didn't even acknowledge my question. Then I asked what I really wanted to ask him, "Dad are you deciding to go on to heaven?" He didn't answer, he just looked at me peacefully.

I turned back to Mom. She stood up and said it was time for her to go. "But I'll miss you," I said desperately crying.

"Miss me then." She said with her feistiest tone, "But I'm all right and everything is going to be just fine. The veil between heaven and earth is very thin." This was a familiar thing for her to say about the death of a loved one. I didn't want to be comforted by her words, but I was anyway. She pointed towards a large red curtain that had to be three stories high and walked towards it. She disappeared behind it waving and saying, "I love you, buggy!" That was the name only she and Dad called me—I had been a bug eater in my toddler years.

When I turned back around, Dad was missing. I started down that hallway to find him.

Let me reiterate here, that hospital is a very familiar space to me. I've been there multiple times over the past 21 years. My daughter was even born there. I had a great understanding of where all the wards and rooms are, especially the ICU. So, when I started down the hallway, I knew I was headed towards the cafeteria. I asked a woman if she knew where Dad was, and she said, "Yes. I'll take you to where he is.

As I followed her down the hallway, she was wearing scrubs and a mask, but she had perfect eyebrows. You know, the kind that are probably tattoos. She kept reassuring me that she was taking me to the right place. Everything was unfamiliar. I went down hallways that were under construction and restricted. Then she pointed towards a glass-brick wall and said, "Sit in there." Behind that glass-brick wall was an empty waiting room. I sat, looked around. Then felt compelled to return to the lobby.

Trying to get back to the lobby, I went down a completely different hallway and wound up in the same place I had left Mom and the veil/curtain was still there. I saw Dad. He was walking toward the curtain that Mom had gone into.

From somewhere deep in my spirit, I shouted with thunderous force, "The Apostle of the Lord entering heavens gates! Go with joy, Apostle David Roland Robinson!" And from behind the curtain there was such a clamorous praise that went up to God. Dad's voice shouted above them all, "GLORY TO GOD! WHOO!"

I woke up crying. I tried not to wake everyone in the house. I went and hid in my closet and just wept. When I composed myself, I told five people my dream: my husband; my sister, Brenda; my two adult children Mackenzie and Stephan; and my best friend, Pastor Charlene Parker Blue. I told them in even more detail than what I have relayed here.

And It Came to Pass...

At 4:30 A.M. on April 8, I woke up and brushed my teeth. It was a strange thing for me to do at 4:30 in the morning. It was like I was on autopilot. I realized that something was off in the house. I laid back down and then heard an unfamiliar sound. It was Dad calling for help.

I came to his room to help him, and he was ash-white and weak. Even at this, he didn't want me to call for an ambulance. But I did anyway. While waiting for the EMTs to arrive I changed his shirt because he had vomited. There was blood in it, both fresh and what looked like coffee grounds.

When the EMTs arrived, he resisted going to the hospital, but I showed him the vomit with blood on his shirt and begged, "Dad this is very concerning, please go." The EMT said, "Mr. Robinson, that is VERY concerning."

Dad reluctantly accepted their help, and they took him to the hospital. When I walked into the ER it was like I was back in that dream. They allowed me in the room with him for a minute to answer questions and then they asked me about his DNR (do not resuscitate). I told the doctor asking me, "He said to do everything you can, but if his heart stops then let him go to Jesus and his Nancy." I was numb saying it.

The doctor turned towards Dad just as the nurse asked him the same question. Dad said the same thing, "Do all you can, but If my heart stops, let me go to Jesus and My Nancy."

They made me leave the room because they needed to put a mainline into his neck to give him blood. He was bleeding internally. They took me to a new waiting room... it looked almost exactly like the one in my dream where mom was sitting on black the sofa. From that moment I was walking in the dream/vision I had seen. I stayed on the phone with my sister, Brenda, who was on her way as fast as she could come. I kept telling her to hurry and reminded her of the dream (her ability to get from Georgia to Oklahoma in record time was a miracle in itself). I left it to her to contact all the family. It was an hour before they let me back in the room with him and they had given him 6 units of blood and 2 units of plasma. Someone told me that it was probably half his blood volume.

He was alert and able to talk to me the entire time. He kept telling me that everything was fine and that he was going to be fine. He said he still had things to do and many things to live for.

When they took him for an MRI, they said he would be going to the ICU and then emergency surgery. I knew that the ICU was on the 4th floor because I'd been there with Mom several times. It was next to oncology. But as I headed there a nurse who was going on break asked if I knew where the new ICU was. I didn't and she told me to follow her. I kept gasping as I followed her because she had perfect eyebrows and was wearing the same scrubs and mask I had seen in my dream.

She asked me if I was ok. I told her I was just feeling overwhelmed by everything happening. That was not even a lie.

She took me towards the cafeteria and down a long and winding hallway to a waiting room behind glass bricks. "This just opened recently, it's very new." She said as she pointed for me to sit in the room that still smelled of fresh paint. I took a picture and sent it to my sister. "Do you remember what I said I saw in my dream? I'm walking it out right now! You need to hurry. Dad is going home to Jesus and mom."

When dad came from his MRI one doctor had said emergency surgery would be taking place at 9:00 A.M. Then another doctor came into the room. He was kind but direct. "Mr. Robinson, you are bleeding internally. Your liver is failing from lack of blood flow, and your stomach and upper intestines are ischemic (dead). We are going to put a tube into your stomach through your nose to relieve the pressure and try to restore blood flow to your liver and stomach. It is most commonly fatal, but let's be in our prayers that you are one of the few that do survive this type of internal injury."

The look in my eyes must have spoken volumes because dad looked at me and said, "Don't be bitter." That was him telling me that he was going to go to Jesus and Mom.

You see, the week after mom had died, he'd fallen on his stomach. He refused to go to the ER when the EMTs arrived. From that time until this he had been having problems with digestion which made his belly swell twice its normal size and he would have to force himself to burp to relieve pressure. I begged him to call the doctor or let me take him to the ER. He refused every time. The point is, that fall was the initial injury that led to his condition.

When they put the tube down his nose into his stomach, blood came gushing into the receptacle. They gave him pain medication and something to try to stop the bleeding. The blood still draining into the receptacle was a signal to me that the medicine that they'd given him, and the plasma were not going to work to stop the bleeding. He had been on an irreversible blood thinner for several months. Because Covid restrictions limited his ability to go to the lab for blood tests. The "new" blood thinner did not need a monthly blood test, but the downside was that it has no known reversing agent. In case of a bleeding emergency, options are limited with a low chance of success to stop the bleeding.

I sat in the chair near his bed and nodded off. During the next three hours, three other people coded in rooms around us. They try to keep the sound down by white noise in the room, but it is hard when you hear a wife or mother begin to wail. Although it was very muffled, I could still hear it.

At around noon Dad began talking to mom. At first, I thought he was talking to me, but he was alert and talking to Mom beside his bed. He was whispering, trying not to wake me up. He said, "but Brenda. ...but Brenda." And then he laid his head back and said, "WHOO Glory!" and smiled. I sat quietly and listened. He lifted one hand and said it again. I asked him if he needed anything, He opened his eyes, completely alert and aware, "I am fine. Don't worry about me. Linda Bug, I am fine. Everything is all right."

Let me mention here that the ICU room Dad was in is the same room Mom was in when she passed. Do with that what you will.

At 12:09 P.M. I got a text from my husband for me to come and get my meds. He had brought them to me at the door of the ER lobby.

Covid-19 restrictions did not allow him in. I got up and walked to Dad, took his hand, and told him, "Dad, I have to go take my meds. I haven't taken them, and I know my blood pressure is high. I can feel it."

He opened his eyes and looked into mine, clear, alert, and aware, "I am fine. Don't worry about me. You take care of yourself. I love you. I love all my kids. Tell them that. I am fine. Don't worry." Then he closed his eyes, laid back his head, and said, "Whoo glory!" and squeezed my hand.

"Brenda will be here by 6. But I'll only be gone a few minutes." I kissed his hand and his cheek. I smelled the sweet sick smell of the blood in his mouth. He opened his eyes and reiterated, "I am fine. You take care of yourself. Whoo Glory!"

When I left the room, I asked the nurse if everything was ok enough for me to go get my meds and get something to eat. She said to me, "He's doing really well. His vitals are very strong. Much better than when he got here." It was in no way a promise, just the facts. But I thought to myself that he would not go for a day or two. I thought he had more time, so I decided to go ahead and leave. But to get back to the ER where my husband was waiting for me, I had to take a completely different hallway, just like in my dream. While I was walking down the hallway, I was remembering the dream and I tried to remember what I had said when Dad entered heaven beyond the veil. I said it out loud, "The apostle of the Lord entering heaven's gates! Go with joy, Apostle David Roland Robinson!"

I reached my husband at the ER door. I took my meds and got in the car with my husband. He took me down the road a little way to get a burger because I have to have food on my stomach with my meds.

At 12:20 the nurse called me and told me that Dad's heart had stopped. When we got his death certificate back, he had passed at 12:13, before I had even gotten out of the hospital. As I was walking down that hallway, when I spoke those words, he was entering heaven and there was great rejoicing! HALLELUJAH!

I called Brenda and told her dad had passed. We were both grief-stricken.

Later, when I told her about dad talking to mom in the hospital room and him saying to her, "...but Brenda, but Brenda." She told me that Mom had come to her in a dream—just as she had done to me—and told her, "Do not call Dad back from heaven. Do not keep him. Do not raise him from the dead. Let him come to me and Jesus." She knew Brenda so well. If she did not have that directive Dad may have died at 12:13pm but he would have been resurrected at 6:30pm when she arrived in the room. I do not doubt that.

I still am grateful for that dream/vision of mom. The Lord knew I needed to have the reassurance that the events of the day that Dad went to heaven "to Jesus and his Nancy" was the way God had planned it. I'm thankful for the people I told beforehand as a witness to the dream so that it is confirmed and cannot be passed off as a grief-stricken fake memory. It gave me peace as I walked through the valley of the shadow of death with Dad. I had no fear, only dread...I was alone there and was already heartbroken from Mom's passing. My adult children, Mackenzie and Stephan, came and surrounded me, gave me strength. They helped me gently grieve as I sat in the room with Dad's lifeless body. The Lord does all things well! Hallelujah!

Personal Prophecy

And if I have prophetic powers (the gift of interpreting the divine will and purpose), and understand all the secret truths and mysteries and possess all knowledge, and if I have [sufficient] faith so that I can remove mountains, but have not love (God's love in me) I am nothing (a useless nobody).

1 Corinthians 13: 2 (AMPC)

"As the snow and rain that fall from heaven do not return until they have accomplished their purpose, soaking the earth and causing it to sprout with new life, providing seed to sow and bread to eat. So also will be the word that I speak; it does not return to me unfulfilled. My word performs my purpose.

Isaiah 55:10-11 (TPT)

God Saw Me Praying

Prophecy is a powerful tool in the Kingdom of God. It is not fortune-telling. It isn't a person standing up and saying, "Someone with a 'g' in their name is struggling and God said to you, 'breakthrough, breakthrough, breakthrough!' If that's you, bring a $20 bill down to the front and let me lay my anointed hands on you.'" That kind of thing is witchcraft and manipulation.

Real prophecy is accurate, specific, and irrefutable. It doesn't always manifest immediately, but a real prophecy will come to pass without fail!

Fourteen and Fed Up

The first prophecy ever given to me from someone other than Dad is a very interesting story. I was fourteen at the time, we still lived in Atlanta. Dad had decided to do a 3-day Thanksgiving Camp-meeting and have speakers from around the country. One of the speakers was a woman by the name of Rev. Doris Rycroft. She and her husband Haskell were founding members of the great organization, The Independent Assemblies. Doris Rycroft has a powerful testimony in her own right and was raised from the dead by Haskell at one time in their younger days of ministry. At the time of this writing, Haskell has graduated to heaven, but Rev. Doris is still with us.

That Thanksgiving Camp-meeting was a bust. Hardly anyone from outside our church showed up. The church members were salty because they didn't get their family Thanksgiving and there were bad attitudes dancing around that place like turkeys on crack. The women were being especially brutal, in my opinion. One lady was so caustic to her husband, she humiliated him, and he just cried. I was 14 and watching all this strife.

My parents had their share of strife as well. Yes, we lived in the miraculous, but we also lived in the 1980s. That era was very hard on ministers and their families. It was a full-out attack from all sides.

On the first day of the meeting, the speakers were good. They preached and encouraged. They took up offerings—people were trying to save for Christmas. Women were ragging on their husbands for giving in every offering to every speaker. I'm telling you, you could feel the daggers coming from these women. At the pot-luck meals I had to help in the kitchen, and they were talking so badly about their husbands I couldn't stand to listen. I volunteered for garbage duty with Sam Greene ('Uv My Dog'). He wasn't the best conversationalist, but I didn't mind talking about his dog and his Christian albums, anything to get out of those women's petty pity party.

That night, exhausted from the work and disillusioned by all of the strife in families (including my own) that I had been exposed to, I lay in bed crying. "God, there has to be a better way. I want to get married someday, but I don't want to make my husband cry in public like 'so and so'. I don't want to be miserable and wish my husband harm... her husband is a good man. He works hard and brings home all his money and she is hiding credit card bills from him." I tell you, when I was praying, I was naming names and spilling the tea to God in graphic detail. I went to sleep crying into my pillow. I was 14. I was dramatic.

I could not tell you what Rev. Doris Rycroft preached. I do remember her telling how she knew the voice of God from a little girl and that we can hear and know his voice too. She invited everyone to the front to have hands laid on them. She went down the line praying for people. When she got to me, she stopped. I had my eyes closed and hands raised. She said, open your eyes, daughter of God.

So, I did.

Her dark eyes looked into mine and she said, "THUS SAITH THE LORD!" In a booming voice. Everyone looked at me and the whole building was at a complete holy hush. Even the babies stopped crying.

"I heard you in the nighttime, yay, even last night crying on your bed unto me," Then the Lord quoted me almost word for word. But instead of using names, The Rev. Doris Rycroft said, "you have cried out to me, 'This one, yay, hath made her husband cry'" and pointed in the direction of the perpetrator without taking her eyes off me, "and that one, yay, hath wished her husband harm... hiding credit card bills and purchases from him. Thou has said he is a good man. And I say to thee, thou hast said rightly!" still never averting her gaze but pointing at the guilty party, and down the line until all six women I had named to God was standing still as stone and red-faced. "You have said to me that you don't want to be like them, and I say, Yay! Thou art my daughter, my handmaiden, the apple of my eye! You will not be like these ones. For I have set you apart, and I have set your husband apart. You shall not date around. You shall not have strife. But I will prepare you and I will prepare him, and you will meet at an appointed time, and you will come together, and marry, and not fight, nor be in strife, but you will agree to walk together towards me. For I, the Lord God have ordained it."

I tell you, for months and months after that prophecy every woman in the church acted like their husbands were superman. They complemented them and swooned over them. The men of the church treated me like a princess, while the women feared me.

Prophecy fulfilled.

When I was 28 years old, I met the wonderful man that is my husband, Donald Pendley. Every word of the Rev. Doris Rycroft's prophecy to me has come to pass. Would you believe that he was a member of Rev. Doris Rycroft's church, Rays of Life, in Lexington, Oklahoma at the time she prophesied to me? I didn't know that when I met him. I had, however, heard about him a few weeks before this prophecy because he had written to a friend and she showed me the letter. I asked her why she would crush on my brother when she had someone like that back home. She said they were just friends—he had dated her sister one time and they were truly just friends. I never imagined how God was giving me clues about my future. It only took another 14 years for it to come to pass. We met in May 1998—I acted like I was not impressed, but he scared the taters out of me. I tried everything in my power to avoid him.

One day I answered the phone for my sister-in-law because her hands were busy changing my niece's diaper blowout. I usually never answer other people's phones. It was HIM!

The whole time he was talking to me I knew he was going to ask me out. I kept saying in my mind, "No! Thousand times, No! And did I mention, NO?! Well, let me say, No." But when he asked me, my mind is saying "NO...!" but my mouth said, "Sure..." and then I did the flirty girl giggle! I was mortified!

Our first date was September— it was my first date ever. He was my first everything from handholding to kissing. We were Married on December 3rd of that same year.

True to God's word, we don't argue. In any disagreements, we turn to the Word of God and find out what He says, and then we agree that He is right, and we are wrong. My husband has never hit me... except that one time he was riding his bike and he held out his hand to flirtatiously slap my keister as he rode by. I felt the flesh of my keister wrap around his fingers when he connected. I had a purple hand-shaped bruise on my left buttock for weeks. He still feels guilty about it.

He's never called me anything but beautiful and kind words, never given me any reason to doubt his fidelity, although some shady women have tried to latch on to him a time or two. He has been a hard worker. He allowed me to care for my elderly, disabled parents for seven years and not work outside of the home. We have three beautiful children together. Two from our own bodies and one that was prophesied in our 30s that came into our arms when we both had reached our 50s.

Each of our children was prophesied into our lives. But they are still growing in their faith and are not wanting their personal lives on blast. I respect their wishes. Suffice it to say that we knew they were coming, we knew their names and their gender before any Dr's test could tell us, and we knew that God had His hand on them with a purpose to fulfill in His good time.

Our third baby is still in the process of taking our name, so her prophecy cannot be included in this book until all is fulfilled. She is 4 years old at the time of this writing and we have had her for 3 of those 4 years.

When God sends a prophet to tell you something, it will fully come to pass.

> "...also will be the word that I speak; it does not return to me unfulfilled. My word performs my purpose.
>
> *Isaiah 55:11 (TPT)*

LOOK OUT!

I don't go looking for people to prophesy to me. I don't go to services expecting a Word from the Lord other than the sermon that is preached. I don't let just anyone "speak into my life." People who are immature in the Lord or are dabbling in manipulation are out there, willing to lay hands on anyone. Some of them will say, "give me twenty bucks and I'll send you a prophecy." Don't participate in that! That is witchcraft!

Just because they have a "prophet" or "prophetess" title before their name does not mean they are of God or give them the authority to speak over your life. You have to discern what spirit they are of—light or darkness.

Remember back in the section about demons where the lady that puked frogs was speaking in tongues but it was a religious spirit and not the Holy Spirit? She was a fortuneteller. One of her "mediums" was Jesus. She used the name of Jesus as an entrance into people's lives to insert demonic forces.

We have to guard the door of our hearts.

Don't go searching for prophecy. Instead, go searching for God through his word and prayer. Ground yourself in a Bible Believing, Bible-practicing church. Pay attention. Inspect the fruit of the people prophesying. If they leave chaos in their wake, then don't let them lay hands on you. If they don't study the Bible, then they cannot "rightly divide the word of truth."[35]

Build your relationship with the Lord and you will recognize His voice and know when the voice is an imposter.

The true Word of the Lord may take time to come to pass. The Lord may be telling you about what is coming in a future season—like prophecy to me at the age of 14 then meeting my husband at 28, or Joseph at 13 dreaming of things that came to pass in his 40s. Prophetic words come to pass in God's timing. We are still looking forward to the fulfillment of Prophetic words that came over 4000 years ago from the Prophet Daniel.

James 1:3-4 (AMPC)

3 Be assured and understand that the trial and proving of your faith bring out endurance and steadfastness and patience. 4 But let endurance and steadfastness and patience have full play and do a thorough work, so that you may be [people] perfectly and fully developed [with no defects], lacking in nothing.

We must trust God's timing and, in the meantime, prepare for the fulfillment of his sure Word. God's word will not return to him

---

[35] 2 Timothy 2:15 **Study** to shew thyself approved unto God, a workman that needeth not to be ashamed, rightly dividing the word of truth.

without manifesting the thing it was sent to establish in the earth in its proper time.

A Manager by Next Week

As I mentioned before, my Husband, Donnie, was not raised in church and didn't have the experience of knowing what personal prophecy is. The first time he went to a church as a young teen where they spoke in tongues, he and his friends sat there stifling snickers and giggles. It was an introduction to something that would play a large part in his future. By the time he was an older teen and young adult he had decided that Church was something he wanted in his life and God was something he was hungry for. I am forever grateful for the Pastor Buck Jordan and his wife Juanita for taking him under-wing and introducing him to Jesus and for Rays of Life Church in Lexington, Oklahoma for being his first experience in the "Family of God."

Donnie was in high school when he took his first job washing dishes at the local pizza place. It was a job he took because his family was struggling financially for reasons that should never have happened. Their family had extreme insecurity of food and shelter. The stress of those times was so bad that he could hardly keep food down. Working at the pizza place he was able to have a meal and help with the bills. He felt honored to help.

He enjoyed the job and soon was moved from dishes and cross-trained to all positions until he became a key-holder and shift leader. But he had never seen himself as more than an hourly worker.

One Sunday, Pastor Buck was preaching and in the middle of his sermon stopped. He looked at Donnie and called him up and gave him a lengthy prophecy. The main point of it was not to be afraid of promotion, that the Lord had given him an anointing to be in management, and to take the promotion when they offered it to him.

Donnie loved Pastor Buck (who has since gone on to heaven) and accepted that it might be a word from God, but he had no knowledge that anyone was thinking about promoting him. As a matter of fact, there were people who had worked there longer who were in line for that type of promotion long before him.

In less than two weeks the Area Director came and sat down with Donnie and told him that they thought he was management material. They wanted to promote him, but he was on salary with health benefits and a 401K option. At the time and for his family, which was a great leap forward.

About 10 years later, in 1998, Pastor Buck and Juanita took my mom and I out for pizza to the place where Donnie was managing. We met in March and married that December—the fulfillment of Rev. Doris Rycroft's prophecy to me 14 years earlier.

"Helping Others in Strange Ways"

The last prophecy given by our Pastor in Waycross, Ga before he passed away was to Donnie and myself. In the middle of his las sermon he stopped and pointed at Donnie and me and said these words, "Strange ways." Then he started to go back to his sermon and stopped again, "Strange ways, you will help your family in strange ways. You will be a blessing to them in strange ways. You will strengthen them, in strange ways. You will bless them and bless them in strange ways.

This prophecy is a strange one, and we don't believe that is has completely come to pass, but we have helped family out in strange ways. Caring for mom and dad at home rather than in an assisted living facility was strange at the time and rather new in the scheme of life. There are other ways that I could point out that seem strange, like seeing a video on a particular subject the day before and then, while speaking to a family member about something they were going through I had the answer from that video.

This prophecy has not been completely fulfilled so I don't have a complete telling of what it means. I wanted to add it to the book because that is the true nature of prophecy, we don't always see everything, we may not even see the fulfillment of it completely in our lifetime. It may just be that this prophecy is the paving stone for the next generation to find the thing that gives them the way to their own life fulfillment.

Rest assured, though, my husband and I are ever alert to the Holy Spirit when it comes to helping others, and when He guides us to do things or say things that seem "strange" our steps are more confident because of this true word from God.

Let His Miracles Overtake You!

Miracles Everyday

I do not walk around on this earth floating in an aura of tranquility. My laundry is half done. My dog peed on the carpet and I'm angry at him. My dishes need to be put away. I'm in my 50's and I have a kid in Pre-K and my body feels every second of those 50 years, craving just one night of uninterrupted sleep. I take high blood-pressure meds, and meds for type II diabetes. I work from home as a customer service rep taking insurance claims. I feel like I have more to give, just not the strength to give it, and that I have yet to fulfill my calling. You can't get more normal.

What has set me apart from the normal is that I acknowledge the supernatural every day. No, I don't blame the devil for every little thing, neither do I think that God is to blame for everything, but I am keenly aware that the ebb and flow of life is influenced by the unseen, daily.

Something I love to do is to read about physics—not psychics! You know, quantum physics, Einstein, Michio Kaku, string theory, etc. Those subjects are exciting to me because the more science delves into energy, matter, dark matter, and anti-matter the more science tells us that there is more out there than what we can see. That there are places, forces, lights, darknesses, that cannot be sensed by analog human senses, but can be detected by the influence they have on what is seen. Yes, its deep, but it's also so common it has been happening everywhere since the beginning of time when God said, "Light Be!"

Supernatural forces in the world are working beyond our analog human senses but we are first spirit beings, with a soul, housed in a body—so our spirit can connect to the spiritual kingdoms (good or bad) as well as we can see spiritual influences in the world and on people without having to see spirits with our eyes. We see their effects on people like Einstein saw the effects of gravity on light, bending starlight around the heavenly bodies in the sky to be seen during a full solar eclipse.

As mom's we can sense when something is tugging on our children, even if we haven't laid eyes on them for days. I know when my children are struggling. I know it in my spirit. It makes me pray, text or make a phone call. It puts me on high alert.

I'm not a special being on the planet, I was just brought up believing in the supernatural and miracles. When you understand that these forces are out there, and that God is an everyday God, then you walk differently, see differently, act differently.

After I learned about gravity in first grade, when a cup fell and shattered, I understood on some small level why it happened. I didn't have to think about it again, I didn't have to waste time on asking why. I understood that gravity had pulled the cup down as a natural force. The same can be said of miracles, when you know they happen, that there are spiritual forces and principles at play, you stop asking all of the endless toddler "WHY" questions and begin to trust in the spiritual principals at play.

The more you know about God and his Kingdom of light, the more you walk confidently when things seemingly go wrong.

I admit, I have been so **angry** at God for the way Mom died. It wasn't fair how she was mistreated in the rehabilitation home, a sadistic medication nurse withholding pain meds from her and torturing her with pain. Mom did not die from the Covid-19 in her system, she died from not having proper medication that caused her to seize. She shouldn't have suffered like that. NOT MY MIRACLE BELIEVING MOM!

But she did. We were kept from her from the time she went into rehabilitation to the time she passed because of Covid-19 restrictions. I resented that—it is still a cause of emotional pain and I weep every time I think about anyone being cruel to my mom.

Yet, she had already told me she was leaving. The night before she had the first long seizure, she called all of her children and spoke to them. She told me she was done and that she was tired. I said I would bring her home as soon as her quarantine was over—she was due to be out of quarantine the next day. But she was done. She only gained consciousness one more time in the ICU and I begged her to stay and even bribed her with powdered donuts if she decided to live and come home.

You see, mom had already gone to heaven once. I was a baby and she had pneumonia. Her lungs collapsed at home, no one knew, I lay in a little apple crate beside the bed, and she lifted out of her body and went to heaven. After some time there, Jesus told her she could stay. She almost said yes. Her mother's heart outweighed the glory, "But what about my children?" she asked Jesus. He smiled and she was immediately back in the room where she had died standing over her body... but that is another book she told me to write.

She came back and raised us kids. She said that she would live to see all of her grandchildren. And she did. My little Lilly is her last grandchild. She was assured by God about that. But think...if Mom had decided to stay in heaven. This book would have no chance of having been written. She wouldn't have lived to tell me the stories. She would have never taught me about the family legacy of supernatural multiplication of food. I never would have known about the ministry of angels to the people of God and I would have absolutely, without a doubt never have written this book.

That day that Mom called all us kids and said her goodbyes I believe that she had chosen to go home to Jesus and prepare the way for Dad. I think part of it was to release me to move on and finish this book for you. To free me to tell the story without worrying about Dad's disappointment that the words don't convey the glory of the actual day that it happened, or Mom's grammar policing, or, most importantly, me hiding behind them as obligations to say, "I'm just too busy." Those are the negative carnal influences that, if you don't know their pull and effects, you don't resist them.

"What do you mean, carnal influences?" You ask. In the parable of the seed and the Sower, in Matthew 13:22 Jesus told his disciples,

> *"He also that received seed among the thorns is he that heareth the word; and the care of this world, and the deceitfulness of riches, choke the word, and he becometh unfruitful. (KJV)*

This is what was happening to me. I had received the seed of the Word of God regarding miracles. But the cares of the world were choking the life out of the message so it wouldn't bear fruit. That fruit is you believing, walking, living in, and testifying of miracles.

I wanted mom to walk in a miracle and walk out of that rehab facility like she had so many times before but she was done. She had finished her course and she chose to go home to Jesus. That was her miracle, walking through the gates of heaven for a second time, seeing God on his throne again, running to embrace the children she had placed in heaven decades before, embracing her baby brother who had tragically died young, walking to her new home in heaven and seeing her dad, and finally knowing his name.

It wasn't my choice to make. It wasn't the way I wanted it to happen. But now that grief is subsiding, I am determined to do the last thing she told me to do; because she lived a life here on earth, with all its heartaches and sorrows, by choice, to raise me up to carry on the legacy for my family and others. Her last conversation with me she told me **FINISH THE BOOK!**

Just so you know. I just did.

Last Words

These are not my last words on miracles or supernatural life, but they are the last words of this book. I want to emphasize to you that the spirit realm is very real. Heaven and hell and those who occupy them are very real. Heaven is not promised just because you know about it. Just like hell and all its forces are out there to keep you in fear, blinded, or indifferent to the spiritual kingdoms that are at war.

Whose side are you on? Do you know?

I want you to know, without a doubt, that you are on the winning side.

If you'd like to know too, you can pray this prayer or not. Whether you do or not will be the determining factor of a life of faith and victories in hard-fought battles or a life of fear and uncertainty about this age we are in and the ages yet to come.

Father God,

I come to you today and ask you to apply the blood of Jesus, the sacrifice of himself that he gave on the cross, to me. Apply the blood to me to cover me and my sin. I want to be your child, in your family, taking on your name and nature. Forgive me for anything and everything I've done that separated me from you. From here on out help me to live. Give me wisdom, fill me with your Holy Spirit, and teach me the way of your Kingdom; because I have learned that You, oh Lord, are GOOD, and Your MERCY ENDURES FOREVER!

FOR THE LORD IS GOOD AND HIS MERCY ENDURES FOREVER!

About the Author:

Linda Pendley is the wife of Donald Pendley. At the time of this writing, they have three children: Mackenzie, Stephan, and Lilly. The former two children are adults, and the latter is in Pre-K.

Linda began her ministry career at 10 years old teaching Sunday School to toddlers and becoming a fully ordained minister at the age of 18. She has literally dedicated her life to the Gospel.

She has been published in CharismaLife Children's Church Curriculum, as well as an Editorial in CharismaLife Magazine and served on the magazine's reader's advisory board for one year.

Linda is an avid speaker, worship leader, and encourager whose ministry is heavy on the power of God in modern times. She has also taken up the mantle of prayer-warrior from her family legacy. She is dedicated to chronicling the miracles in modern times, but also seeking out of print "lost manuscripts" of awakenings, revivals, and moves of God and bringing them back in print form to the church through her publishing company, CenterMark Publishing.

Linda's next venture in publishing is to become a writing coach for ministers so that the legacy of testimonies in their lives can be the footprints left to the next generation enabling them to follow in the faith.

You can contact Linda on her website:

lindapendleyministries.com

Made in the USA
Middletown, DE
03 June 2024